# COACHING

In The Workplace

# COACHING In The Workplace

Principles and practice of coaching for high performance in the workplace

---

*This book can transform ordinary managers to dynamic leaders.*

First Edition

# Nkem Paul

NKEM PAUL

**Coaching In The Workplace: Principles and practice of coaching for high performance in the workplace, First Edition**

Copyright © 2014 by Nkem Paul

All rights reserved. No part of this book may be used or reproduced by any means, graphics, electronic, or mechanical, including photocopying, recording, taping or by any information storage retrieval system without the written permission of the publisher except in the case of brief quotations embodied in critical articles and reviews.

The author of this book does not dispense medical advice or prescribe the use of any technique as a form of treatment for physical, emotional, or medical problems without the advice of a physician, either directly or indirectly. The intent of the author is only to offer information of a general nature to help you in your quest for emotional and spiritual wellbeing. In the event you use any of the information in this book for yourself, which is your constitutional right, the author and the publisher assume no responsibility for your actions.

The information presented herein represents the view of the author as of the date of publication. This book is presented for informational purposes only. Due to the rate at which conditions change, the author reserves the right to alter and update his opinions at any time. While every attempt has been made to verify the information in this book, the author does not assume any responsibility for errors, inaccuracies, or omissions.

Published in the United Kingdom

ISBN-10: 1502796791

ISBN-13: 978-1502796790

# CONTENTS

Acknowledgements .................................................. vi
Dedication .............................................................. vii
Introduction ........................................................... ix

## Part I - The Principles of Coaching — 1
1  What Is Coaching? ............................. 3
2  The Benefits of Coaching .................. 11
3  The Manager as a Coach .................. 19
4  The Nature of Coaching .................... 31
5  The Role of a Coach ......................... 45

## Part II - Practicalities of Coaching — 55
6   Effective Questioning ....................... 57
7   The GROW Model ............................ 75
8   Coaching for High Performance ........ 99
9   Self-belief and Motivation ................ 127
10  Overcoming Coaching Barriers ........ 139

## Part III - Coaching for Performance — 149
11  Dynamics of Developing a High
    Performance Team .......................... 151
12  Coaching Teams and Groups .......... 161
13  Giving Constructive Feedback
    and Carrying out Assessment .......... 171
Coaching Toolbox ................................ 184
About The Author ................................ 187

## ACKNOWLEDGMENTS

Looking back to where I came; timid, poor family background, coupled with no proper education; I could only remain grateful to Almighty God, who made it possible for my path to cross with the paths of the following Change Agents: Zig Ziglar, Les Brown, Jim Rhon, Marcia Wieder, Bev James, Audrey Seymour; and my very own personal friends and mentors – John Spence and Alan Barrell. The concept of this book demonstrates how much I have learned from everyone of you so far.

I extend my gratitude to Sir John Whitmore, Timothy Gallwey, and Myles Downey for the wisdom I gained from studying your wonderful books.

I salute my dear wife, Glory Mpamah, for your continued love and support. There's no doubt God has made you my backbone.

I'm ever grateful to Almighty God for life.

# DEDICATION

If you are a change agent, or aspiring to join the league of men and women across the nations, who have found fulfillment in transforming other people's lives, I have written this book for you.

To you, who is constantly seeking for ways to develop your capability and break the boundaries of mediocrity. You, who wants more by improving your performance in career and business, and achieve superior results…;

To my three lovely daughters – Blessing (Mom), Nneka, and Amaka; and two handsome sons – Chidera and Chino: The fear of giving you the best up-bringing that I could afford with your mother has always driven some of the weird decisions that resulted in the awesome goals I've accomplished in my life. This book is dedicated to you!

# Introduction

Why another book in coaching? The answer is simple. Coaching is a proven tool for maximising potentials, through higher levels of awareness. Not only does coaching improve performance, it induces learning and enjoyment, lack of which has made work to become dreadful in many organisations. Think about the tight deadlines, unrealistic goals, ever-increasing drive for efficiency as opposed to effectiveness; the re-engineering processes, restructuring exercises, and expended human resources; all of which tend to sap energy, stifle creativity, instill fear and doubt, and impoverish human beings and the organisations they work.

With the introduction of Coaching in The Workplace, business executives, entrepreneurs and professionals have the opportunity to learn new ways of doing things, acquired the skill to challenge status quo, and support their teams to use their best abilities to maximise performance. Workplace coaching comes with greater opportunity for serious-minded managers to learn and transform from managing to coaching, so their employees can deliver superior outcomes.

In almost twenty years of working in corporate organisations including banks and other financial institutions, I had no single opportunity of being coached by any manager. None of the companies I worked for knew anything about coaching. If they did, it was obviously not important to them at the time.

Some of my employers were more interested in rolling out outrageous monthly targets, with no support system for reaching them. They had no regard for what we did to achieve the targets, and would abuse 'the hell' out of anyone for any little mistakes. Looking back 20 years down the road; it just feels painful to see how great organisations could not make any conscious effort to change its overbearing management style that seemingly destroyed the potentials of their best talents from delivering superior performance.

What if my managers were trained as workplace coaches, so they could in turn coach us to unleash the potentials and creativity already in us?

What if I was coached by my manager to work smarter, overcome my fright, set new goals everyday, discover new possibilities for what I was doing, unleash my creativity, finish my work early, and look forward to another fulfilling day…?

I bet you; the reward would be unimaginable! Relationships would improve, and productivity and profits increased. Think of what would happen if everyone in the organisation was coached to put his or her best talent to work. May be, only the sky would have been the limit for those organisations!

Now that I know the extraordinary power in coaching, I wish I could turn the clock backward, and give a copy of this book to each my managers twenty years ago, to help them learn how to coach their teams to create high performance results.

There is no doubt that the traditional command and control style of managing team is no longer useful for making sustainable progress in organisations that seek to make impact in the marketplace. There is no guarantee though, that reading this book once, or even twice will make you a qualified coach; but one thing is certain. If you read this book and practice the principles and tools that come with it regularly; you will be on your way to making a huge difference in your workplace.

# Part I
# The Principles of Coaching

NKEM PAUL

# Chapter 1

# What Is Coaching?

> *A Coach is a catalyst for CHANGE*

Coaching is the practice of unlocking people's potentials to maximise their performance. It is helping individuals to 'learn and do' as opposed to 'telling them what to do.' An important point here, is that coaching does not rely on people's knowledge, experience, wisdom or insight to be successful. Instead it leverages the capacity of the people being coached (Clients and Coachees), and helps them to think creatively to find the answers they are looking for, by themselves.

Effective coaching is based on the important concept that every individual has the *potential* to *perform*.

Notice the two phrases here:

## Potential | | Performance

The problem is, there is a huge gap between people's potential and how much they can accomplish (performance). For people to be highly effective, this gap between their potential and performance needs to be closed.

It does not really matter the amount of outcome anybody is producing right now, there is always plenty of room for improvement. The gap between potential and performance consists of powerful factors that sabotage people's effort from performing at full capacity. These factors are internal and include fear, self-doubt, anxiety, other people's opinion, and low self-esteem. For the purpose of simplicity, I will refer to these factors as "Inner Conflicts."

## How inner conflicts operate

In my first year as coach, I had tough times coaching entrepreneurs and company CEOs. My major concern was my own perception that convinced me that I was not qualified to coach successful entrepreneurs and company chief executives. I saw this as a big threat to my career and sought help from other coaches to overcome it. Fear, doubt, anxiety or our perception of other people's opinion are all resident in the gap, and strongly oppose our ability to unleash our creativity.

> *Coaches must believe that their clients have hidden in them, the POTENTIALS they need to unleash incredible inventions.*

In order to maximise our potentials and increase productivity, we need to introduce coaching to help us eliminate the impact of inner conflicts, that stand in the way, and also unlock our potentials to maximise our performance.

Coaches believe that their clients are the experts of their own lives. They have incredible power to tap into their creative ability, engage their resources, and accomplish greater goals. The fact that some people don't produce high performance results, does not invalidate the usefulness of coaching. Such people only need to be coached to gain awareness of where they want to be, and take the required steps to reach there.

Until you believe that your clients possess abundant potentials within them to achieve what they want, you may not be able to help them fully. You need to think about the people you coach more in terms of the potentials within them, not on their present performance.

This is the case with some organisations, where managers confine their staff in a box that closes every avenue for them to escape being judged in an appraisal process. In such organisations, appraisal systems are no longer effective and do not produce desired results.

Since we believe that human beings have potentials within them, the question we need to answer is:

1. How then do I know that the potentials are there?
2. How much of the potentials are in there?
3. How do I get the clients to use them?

There is probably no scientific proof to justify that people have potentials, but from my experience of learning to ride bicycle, it is absolutely true that anyone can release his or her potential to *learn* and become an expert in anything, regardless how impossible it might seem initially, if they do not quit.

At different times in our lives, crisis contributes in bringing out our best ability. In a normal circumstance, nobody would dare a live lion. But suppose a lion pounces on someone's child? He or she would definitely give her a fight, at least to rescue the child. The question is; where did the strength to fight a lion come?

The truth is that the potential is always there, it only needs a catalyst to come alive; and in an ideal situation, coaching is the catalyst that gets the best performance out of people.

Coaching can occur formally or informally at anytime, and for any number of reasons. You can coach to motivate your staff, delegate tasks, solve a problem, improve relationships, or strengthen teamwork. But in workplace situations, it is recommended for managers to be less formal so that the conversation can be normal between the manager and staff. In such circumstance, the term coaching may not be used at all.

Regardless of the informality of coaching conversations, managers need to maintain self-awareness, bearing fundamental coaching principles in mind, and asking useful questions to achieve desired outcomes.

For example:

Suppose Janet was working on a number of assignments that was agreed with her manager few days ago. After a while on the task, she needed some clarifications before she could make progress. So she decided to go speak with her manager:

Janet: I've done what we agreed that I should do, but it didn't work.

Manager: Oh no Janet! You must have made a mistake! Go and do it like this....

Obviously, this is not a COACHING conversation!

Consider the following, instead:

Janet: I've done what we agreed that I should do, but it didn't work.

Coach: Right, I'm dashing out to see the managing director. See if you can find the exact problem, and I'll be right back to help you.

Twenty minutes later...

Janet: I got it! It's working okay now.

Coach: Fantastic! What did you do?

Janet: The problem was that I included.... and when I removed it, it worked okay.

Coach: Great; what else was affected by the initial problem?

Janet: Nothing else was affected, I checked.

Coach: You're a genius, well done!

Coaching in the workplace can be a very useful tool for supporting and empowering individuals to take responsibility for their actions and change their outcomes. In organisations where people do not take ownership of their actions, productivity is usually low. Coaching impacts on responsibility and gives employees a sense of ownership for the work they do.

# Chapter 2

# The benefits of coaching

Coaching has multiple benefits to a wide variety of stakeholders. Both the coach, the coachee, and organisations or businesses they work for experience tremendous turnaround when they go through the process.

Below are some of the key benefits coaching can bring.

## High performance

As you must have heard already, coaching brings the best performance out of people. Weather applied to life, business, career, relationship, health and wellness, or finance, coaching results are phenomenal. Coaching leaves people and organisations more improved, more productive, more profitable, and more fulfilled.

## Development and growth occurs

The bottom line for a coaching result is growth. People develop quickly from one stage of awareness and knowledge to another, with only a little effort on the part of the coach. This has been demonstrated in people's ability to set audacious goals, and taking responsibility in executing carefully selected action steps to achieve them.

## A better learning approach

Corporate training and development programs are good sources of skills acquisition. But coaching takes human capital development to an ultimate high level, and the results are sustainable. People learn faster with coaching, and apply their learning much easily in real life situations.

## Relationships are improved

One of the profound tools used in coaching is questioning. The act of asking questions and receiving answers helps to improve relationships between coaches and their clients, which telling, giving advice or instruction do not, and will not create. In addition, two fundamental things happen when clients answer their coach's questions. First of all, trust is built, and secondly, hope is restored for the future. These factors are important for achieving improved levels of performance.

## Work environment and quality of life is improved

In addition to trust, coaching helps in creating a vibrant safe environment for people to work. This occurs as individuals and teams are coached to work together to achieve their goals. People feel safe to support one another as opposed to competition. This act of benevolence and celebration of team successes in the organisation ultimately creates a healthy working atmosphere for everyone to thrive.

## More time for managers and leaders

When people are coached weather in business or workplace environment, they take more responsibility for what they do, and become more accountable for the outcomes they produce. As a result of the rapid growth of awareness they experience, and their ability to take on more responsibilities, managers have more time to focus on strategic functions, while delegating operational roles to team members.

## People become more creative and innovative

A coaching environment stimulates creativity and innovation. It helps people from different backgrounds and levels of responsibility to brainstorm way forward for their projects and find solutions for the best performance.

## Better use of people's talent

Managers don't have any better idea of their team's abilities until they engage in series of coaching conversations with them. Coaching therefore helps to discover hidden potentials in people, and empowers them to put their best ability to achieve what they want.

## Proactivity takes place

People who are coached, are more aware of what they want to do, when they want to do them, and how to do them. They no longer wait to be told; instead they simply take action. They are proactive, and produce incredible outcomes as a result.

## People adapt quickly to change

When people go through coaching for a long period, change becomes a normal way of life to them. They understand that no one could make any further progress in life unless they embrace change. In the workplace, they learn to adapt with changes in technology, global innovation, communication, economic uncertainty and social instability that often affect the marketplace.

## Motivation is induced

Coaching helps people to gain awareness of the factors that drive their actions, and releases the power within them to consistently focus on increasing their source of power and inspiration. The awareness and joy of knowing that you have the ability to solve your own problems makes you unstoppable.

## Improved Organisational culture

Coaching principles and tools reinforce good management and leadership. This contributes in creating high performance culture within and outside the workplace. Any organisational culture, which is not supported by effective workplace coaching will probably not achieve its primary objective.

## A life-long skill

After practicing coaching for many years, it normally becomes part of ones way of life. And because coaching is becoming more and more in demand, people find themselves taking up coaching as a new career at the end of their successful career in the workplace.

There seems to be a lot more benefits in coaching than we can think or write about. The bottom line is that organisations that coach their employees are by far performing better than their competitors. Coaching can be powerful for individuals and teams to identify their potentials, discover new skills, overcome their weaknesses and become more effective and more results-oriented.

# Chapter 3

# The Manager As Coach

The terms "coach" and "manager" are two different kettles of fish. Although some managers *claim* to be coaches, we know that tradition has placed on their shoulders, the role of planning, organising, commanding, coordinating, and controlling resources (including human resources) in the most effective ways possible, in order to produce the best results.

The traditional roles give managers the responsibility to tell people what to do, show them how to do them, and punish them if they do them wrongly. To fulfill the function of a coach, managers therefore need to transform from managing to coaching. This is entirely a new skill that must be learned.

As I said in the previous chapters about who a coach is, and the type of relationship that exists between coaches and their clients, coaching skills need to be gradually introduced in the workplace. For coaching to function effectively in the workplace, the relationship between managers and employees must be built on trust, safety, and minimal pressure. This demands that managers should develop empathy, integrity, and detachment; as well as demonstrate willingness to look at things from different perspectives.

The ability to set clear expectations, provide quality and unbiased feedback aimed at improving performance are all part of the game. But the polarity of some managers, especially in their proverbial "carrot and stick" style of management makes the transition a little challenging and less smooth.

In November 2001, I attended a training program organised by my bank. Prior to the training, I had unresolved issues with my manager, and I thought the training provided me the opportunity to seek professional advice from the trainer; moreover as we were training on team building. So I explained my situation to the trainer and asked for his counsel.

Responding, the trainer drew a metaphor that got stuck in my head till date.

He said: "Be careful how you manage the situation with your 'boss' because he holds the "machete" on the base, with your hands on the blade. If he decides to pull the machete, you can be sure what would happen to you." Unfortunately that's the position most managers occupy in some workplaces that makes it highly challenging for their staff to use their best abilities at work.

I believe that managers can learn and apply coaching skills to improve their quality of work, as well as support their staff to deliver extraordinary performance. Nevertheless, senior management needs to create the environment for smooth transition, by introducing coaching as part of its strategic focus within the organisation.

In a good coaching environment, employees need to feel completely safe and confident to express their opinions without pressure or consequence from higher authorities afterwards.

While coaching upholds the "carrot" by way of motivation, encouragement and empowerment, there is absolutely no place for the "stick" or *the "machete"* in a coaching dispensation.

As in every coaching situation, managers need to develop appropriate skills to be able to help their employees become the best they want them to be. In practice the most successful managers and leaders engage the services of external coaches to hold their employees accountable the producing quality results. Even the most experienced coaches have their own personal coaches in different areas of life, career, business or health, who work with them to achieve their different goals.

At the early stage of introducing coaching in the workplace, there is possibility that managers could experience resistance from their staff. This occurs as a result of employee's suspicion of the manager's sudden departure from controlling, to a more humanistic approach of empathy and encouragement.

## The Telling Culture

If you are like me, you probably grew up in environments that conditioned you not to take responsibility for your actions. Majority of us were raised by parents, who told us what we did with no questions asked. We went to schools where teachers were 'gods.' They told us what we did and disciplined us if we dare say no. The situation was the same if not worse in the workplace. So as we too grew up, we could not behave any different from what we learned over the years. We took pleasure in telling others what they should do.

Majority of the world's population has been brought up on this telling culture, and because it forms the foundation of our development, we became very good at it.

For managers in the workplace, the telling habit can be quite challenging to give up because it is easy, fast and cool to execute. Besides, it gives some funny feelings of authority and control when used. But it only stifles initiative and renders human potentials redundant.

In a research by IBM, which was validated by Royal Mail United Kingdom, a group of individuals were divided randomly in three subgroups, each being taught the same thing using different methods. The overwhelming conclusion was evidenced by the dramatic fall experienced in people who failed to "recall" after they were told to do something.

Below is a table showing results from the research:

|  | Told | Told and Shown | Told, Shown and Experienced |
|---|---|---|---|
| Recall after three weeks | 70% | 72% | 85% |
| Recall after three weeks | 10% | 32% | 65% |

Ironically, different managers adopt different styles to management. But regardless of the approach, coaching stands on a different pedestal. It requires change of mindset from autocracy, fire-fighting, and command to support and empowerment. This helps to bring commitment to work.

## Transforming from managing to coaching

> *For things to change you first have to change!* – Jim Rohn

It is simple to transform from managing to Coaching in a workplace. Nevertheless, the simplicity of the process does not make it easy to implement in any way. As in every change situation, commitment is required from managers, who are expected to practice the skills of coaching consistently. They need to first change their ways of thinking, and be able to consider things differently.

Why?

From my experience of coaching entrepreneurs, who are successfully building their own Self-Sustaining Enterprises, the biggest hurdle people may have to overcome in order to make sustainable change is self. Over the years, we grew up to do things in ways that reinforced our personalities and endorsed our self-esteem. In attempt to maintain status quo or protect our personal integrity, we device creative means of resisting changes we do not want. Other people do so because of their personal perception of fear. Generally, anyone can accept change. The problem is that people are only quick to accept changes they initiated. If they did not initiate the change, they resist it.

There are three valid observations about change that hold true:

1. When change is to be made, people in positions of authority often absolve themselves from the need to change themselves first.

2. When we resist change, it's often that we resist the process through which change will come; we do not resist the change at hand.

3. In the workplace, resistance to change is founded on the command and control approach of management.

The change from managing to coaching is a good change. The starting point is to develop a mindset that encourages, empowers, and praises people, rather than *commanding, telling* them what to do, and punishing them.

One of the basic facts that make coaching process simple is the truth that individuals have innate potential to achieve extra-ordinary results, but needs a catalyst to empower and inspire them to just do it.

## The Fear to Transform

Quite often, the Number One fear managers express in transiting from managing to Coaching is lose of control. Many managers fear that they would loose control to their staff through coaching.

This is not true in reality. No one looses control for coaching. Instead, you will need to exercise your control differently by asking powerful questions designed to impact your clients positively, and help them to produce outstanding results. This has been proven to be much more powerful and effective way of exercising control.

Asking the right questions in a simple conversational manner will help your staff to think deeply, make the right choices, and take appropriate steps for the project. In essence, it gives you opportunity to exercise control in a more reasonable way; and to your staff, the freedom to choose what they consider best options for their actions.

Take a look at what transpired between Janet and her Manager on Page 8. Janet was stuck on a project and needed help from her manager. Instead of getting the support she needed to make progress, she was judged.

> *"Oh no Janet! You must have made a mistake! Go and do it like this…"* he said.

Janet's case was a typical circumstance that could have been dealt more effectively with coaching, if only the manager had coaching skill.

## The price of becoming a Coach.

In many business organisations, an average manager spends his or her day putting out fire. Majority do not have proper planning system or strategy for what should done, or areas of development their staff should focus to improve performance.

The secret is that, if you invest quality time in planning and coaching your staff no matter how little every week, you will invariably develop them to take much responsibility that eventually frees you from fighting fire. The more responsibilities your staff take off your shoulder, the more freedom you will have to deal with issues of strategic importance.

As Janet's manager could not identify her inability to move forward with her project as a coaching challenge, there is possibility also that you may miss some coaching opportunities when you start initially. But the process will become clearer as you continue practicing.

The following three situations can guide you in identifying when a coaching opportunity arises.

1. **Time**: If time is of essence in the matter, i.e. if the situation is an emergency or one of crisis, doing it by you could produce the right speed and incredible result at the time.

2. **Quality**: You need to determine if quality is of the essence in the matter. Being "the manager" does not guarantee that you must know everything. If quality is the desirable outcome in any situation, and you have someone in your team who has the skill to deliver the expected quality, such member of the team could be coached to take up the responsibility.

4. **Learning**: If the situation is one that demands for learning to be maximized; for example in delegating a job, or solving a child's homework from school; then coaching will optimize the learning outcome and ensure retention.

In some organisations time, quality, and learning have some degrees of dominance in people's day-to-day activities. Unfortunately, managers seem to give precedence to time at the expense of quality and learning.

## Chapter 4

# The Nature of Coaching

There are two fundamental consequences that occur as a result of coaching. These are **awareness and responsibility**. Gaining awareness and taking responsibility are two direct results of focusing and gaining clarity on the subject matter of coaching.

## Creating Awareness

Awareness gives understanding to information, situation or event, and helps in determining the relevance of the subject matter. In an ideal world, people do not make meaningful contributions to, or take control of situations unless they first gain awareness of facts about the situation. In other words, whatever people are unaware about, controls people.

Awareness is like the ray of an early morning sunshine that falls quite strongly on a garden of plants and flowers. It leaves them with no choice than to grow and blossom. Likewise, when an individual gains awareness over an issue of importance, he or she literally gains clarity of perception on the facts and figures that they didn't know existed. In the course of gaining awareness, learning takes place and the client reaches an "Aha Moment."

The great thing about self-awareness is that, unlike telling, clients are empowered to discover things by themselves. They do this by simply answering questions from the coach, which have been designed to help them think outside the box. This process of awareness leads to self-discovery, and invariably increases confidence.

While we can relate general awareness to the knowledge of what is happening around us, self-awareness is, knowing what we are experiencing, as a result of what is happening around us. It is important to note that with a high level of self-awareness, people can respond to life situations more positively, and quickly too.

## Taking Responsibility

To take responsibility is the second fundamental focus of coaching. Believe me, for coaching to produce desired results, someone must take responsibility for making the decision, or taking the actions that will produce the results. Therefore, **responsibility** is a key element of coaching that has potential to move an individual from simply "knowing" to performance. Every result we experience in life, whether good or bad is a direct response to our responsibility. The whole idea of creating awareness is futile unless someone makes the commitment to an action that translates the awareness to reality.

Responsibility is important for creating high-performance results. Until people are held accountable for what they want, they cannot make a commitment with their time, money and energy towards achieving the results they seek. But if a person truly accepts to take responsibility for his or her thoughts and actions, they would obviously take action to produce the results.

Some times, we attribute people's inability to take responsibility to fear of failure, or disempowering beliefs. While any one of these can be true, it is apparent that great majority of people in the workplace will not take responsibility when they are not given opportunity to make a choice.

It is usual for some managers and leaders to assign responsibility by command or threat. But true responsibility cannot be imposed, ordered or forced. To be effective, responsibility can only be given by choice, and many people will not take responsibility unless they're first given opportunity to choose their outcomes; and whatever choices they choose is entirely up to them.

As coach, part of your roles is to open up the opportunities and support your clients to choose and commit. The idea of exercising control, and manipulating people to do what they don't want to do is counter-productive.

Unfortunately, it is common for the leadership of organisations that operate in this manner to complain about low productivity or lack of responsibility in their teams.

In 2014, the leadership of a small church I belonged in Cambridge once forced its members to pledge large sums of money towards buying a church building. The deadline for redeeming the pledge was three months and by the end of the deadline, only a tiny fraction of members who pledged could redeem their pledges.

What was responsible for the poor performance?

Fair enough.

You may have heard the saying that; "You can only take a horse to the river, but you cannot force her to drink." When leaders and managers compel their followers and staff to take responsibility they did not fully accept, it only sets the pace for mediocrity, which will create suspicion and distrust in a matter of time.

When certain situations arise, many people will choose to answer "Yes" to their managers; not because they meant to say "Yes", but because it was the only response they could afford to make the managers happy. Others would do it out of fear, especially if threat was involved, so as "to avoid trouble." Unfortunately, the same people that answered "Yes" would grumble and resent; the moment the manager or leader goes out.

Although people can take action on imposed responsibility, they will only do it when there is a consequence, an implied threat and repercussion; or as a result of avoiding trouble.

Since the actions are not intentional, performance and result will be suboptimal.

Taking responsibility can be truly effective if managers give employees the opportunity to willingly choose their actions and commit their resourcefulness. When people define their own "right approach" for what they want to achieve, they will take ownership of their actions. And they would choose the best course of actions even if anything goes wrong in the process.

Therefore, choice induces commitment and creativity, which are important for creating high performance results consistently.

Let me go a little deeper to demonstrate this with two examples.

Suppose you are bidding for an important contract, and needed two reams of A4 size papers from the store to print the bidding documents for submission. You then called a member of your team: *"James, could you go to the store and bring two reams of A4 papers? We have to finish printing this bid by close of business today."* Off, James went to the store.

Unfortunately there were no more A4 papers in the store. What did James do? He returned and say to you: *"I have checked the store and there was no A4 paper left."* End of story, but mission still unaccomplished!

What if you had given the team an opportunity to choose their action, instead of telling or commanding them on what to do?

Let's look at the second example.

Suppose you walked to the team and said: *"Hi folks, we need two reams of A$ papers from the store to start printing our bid document. As you know the submission deadline is 5:00p.m today. Who can get the papers from the store for us?"*

I can assure you that if James could not take responsibility to go, someone else in the team, may be Esther might say: *"I'll go for it!"*

Let us assume further that Esther went to the store and did not find any paper; what else could she do? Well, there are a couple of options she could explore. First, she could borrow from her colleagues in other departments. She could as well dash to the stationery store across the road and buy some.

Whatever action Esther decides to take in producing the stationery will be persuaded by the fact that she first made the choice. By not making effort to produce the result would mean letting down her self-esteem which should would not do. So she is willing to explore every available option.

If Esther exhausts all available options and still did not find any; would she not feel let down? Not likely! If Esther could not produce the A4 paper after exploring the options, she would still feel satisfied to have carefully exhausted the options. The next thing that would possibly happen, would be having a brief coaching session, either in group or one-on-one with her manager to explore any options she may not have considered, and find a way forward for the paper.

But what if she bought some from the stationery store across the road? That would have been a wonderful performance, wouldn't it?

Without a doubt, the nature of coaching is to **raise *awareness*** and **create *responsibility*** for maximising potentials, and creating high performance results. These two factors are highly necessary in performing any activity and achieving any goal.

## Qualities of A Good Coach

In our *Teach2Coach training programs*, where we train managers and corporate executives to become workplace coaches, we ask our delegates to tell us the qualities they expect their ideal coaches to posses. Quite often, they come up with a list of great qualities, which include the following:

- ❖ Supportive
- ❖ Active listener
- ❖ Mutual trust
- ❖ Honesty
- ❖ Transparency
- ❖ Patient
- ❖ Excellent communicator
- ❖ Empathy
- ❖ Respect

It is really hard work to articulate the qualities a good coach should possess because great coaches come from different backgrounds, and offer different coaching styles. However, in every successful coaching relationship, it is desirable for coaches to have excellent relational skills.

In a coaching relationship, it is important for the coach to communicate, connect, inspire performance, and achieve result. In exercising these qualities, they also exhibiting other great skills that incidentally sets them apart.

Particularly in a coaching session, two fundamental qualities fall out of *communication;* these are – ability to **ask great questions**, and **listen**. The extent to which coaches develop these two skills determines the effectiveness of their coaching, and the value they create for their clients.

By engaging in quality communications, people gain deeper understanding, develop trust and feel safe to focus on their goals. As a Coach, your relationship with your client can be influenced by a general belief clients are resourceful enough to achieve their goals.

In addition, being a workplace coach means that you need to invest quality time to understand your staff. You have the responsibility to make them fee confident to share their challenges with you and trust you to maintain high level of integrity and confidentiality.

To function effectively as coach, I am going to discuss three factors, which I consider important for coaches to have. These are:

- ❖ Mutual Trust
- ❖ Honesty
- ❖ Transparency or Openness

## Mutual Trust

The whole basis of an effective coaching relationship is built on the foundation of *mutual* trust. Your clients must trust you before they could share their personal information with you. They must belief that you have credibility not to divulge what they consider as *secret* information they share with you, without their consent.

In a typical coaching conversation, clients will share their thoughts, feelings, fears and beliefs with you. As a result, they need 100% safety assurance from you, to be able to express themselves in ways that leave them guiltless. They expect you to listen to them, and acknowledge their situations without having to judge them or make them feel threatened.

I prefer to use the term "mutual trust" because as coaches, we also need to trust our clients to be fully committed to the coaching process, and be as truthful to us, as much as we can be to them. So both parties need to trust one another in order to create powerful results.

## Honesty

In any coaching relationship, it is normal to establish goals and plans of actions, which clients will agree to commit to. Without any doubt, coaches expect their clients to be fully responsible for committing their time and resources in executing the actions that would create the results they are seeking. As it is possible for clients to experience challenges while executing their plans sometimes, coaches expect them to be honest in sharing any difficulties or barriers, which they encounter in the process of executing their actions.

Where a client experiences repeated failure in accomplishing agreed plan of action, it might be a trigger for the coach to check with the client, to ensure that the goals are congruent with their values and beliefs. But before that, the client needs to share his or her challenges or concerns with the coach.

## Transparency or Openness

In a coaching relationship, transparency or openness refers to the coach's ability to encourage, support and facilitate their clients to put all their cards on the table for discussion. Transparency is the by-product of trust.

Openness means that your clients are confident to discuss their issues with you, without holding anything back. It also means that you are actively encouraging them through your questioning skills, to keep their options open and be free to ask questions when they feel stuck.

# Chapter 5

# The Role of A Coach

> *The role of a Coach is not to fix what is broken.*

The objective of this Chapter is to help you identify specific competencies that you need to develop, in your journey towards becoming an excellent workplace coach.

It is crucial to understand who a coach is, be clear about what he or she can do, and set the boundaries for roles they can not perform. But first of all, let me re-emphasize that the primary responsibility of a coach is not to fix problems. Coaches are not problem solvers; the clients are. The role of the coach is to facilitate performance, learning and development for the client.

The effectiveness of a coach's role can be demonstrated in their ability to unlock their clients' potentials, and help them to maximise performance. The coach does this by raising awareness, helping clients to gain deeper understanding of their situations, make informed decisions, and commit their resources.

Primarily, the coach is not to provide solution to the client's problem or fix what they broken. A coach is not a "Miracle Man;" we do not 'bring the dead back to life.' But we can support our clients through facilitation, to find their own solutions. We can help them to dig deeper inside and outside of their minds in search of solution. We can help them to think creatively and create what they are looking for. The process of digging deep helps our clients to uncover series of new options, which they did not consider previously.

Let us examine some of the essential skills coaches are required to develop. The list below has been developed in no particular order of preference and should be given equal consideration.

- ❖ Excellent communication.
- ❖ Use of open-ended questioning tools.
- ❖ Active listening.

- ❖ Repetition, paraphrasing and summarising.
- ❖ Pauses and Silence.
- ❖ Enabling clients to set goals and define their actions.
- ❖ Helping client to explore their values and beliefs.
- ❖ Encouraging clients to explore options and take responsibility.
- ❖ Showing empathy.
- ❖ Maintaining highest level of confidentiality.
- ❖ Keeping clients on track.
- ❖ Praising client's achievement.
- ❖ Acting as sounding board and allowing clients to think through ideas.
- ❖ Challenging and getting clients out of their comfort zone.
- ❖ Facilitating client's understanding of their needs.
- ❖ Maintaining non-judgmental attitude.
- ❖ Ability to manage time effectively in every coaching session.

The list of skills above is not conclusive. I believe that what matters the most is understanding the purpose each skill serves in generating understanding, raising awareness, and inspiring clients in taking action.

In the following sections, I will describe some of the obvious skills, which coaches use whenever they conduct a session.

## Active Listening

The purpose of listening is to hear and gain understanding. That's what creates awareness. As important as listening is in every conversation, it is disappointing to see how many people that listen only with the intention to make a response instead of understanding the speaker first.

At the beginning of a new coaching relationship, some clients may tell their coaches what they want them to hear. The problem is that if you rely totally on what your client says with his mouth, you could instinctively miss what you should hear. As coach, you need to develop the ability to listen actively, and hear unspoken words.

Paying close attention to client's body languages can uncover unspoken words. They manifest through facial expressions, demonstration of hands, or making of eye contacts. They can also be found through observation of changes in client's tonal expression, or shift in their physical composure.

When any of these signs occur, they trigger curiosity in the mind of the coach. The coach then asks a question to challenge the client to open up the issue. It's important to gently challenge the client because, if the issues were left uncovered, they could potentially sabotage them from achieving their goals.

When listening, you need to pay more attention to what is being said, not what you think the client should be saying. You can do this by simply being fully present in the discussion! To be fully present meant to free your mind from any interference from the internal dialogue that takes place in your mind, and focus single minded on the speaker.

Paying close attention to what your clients say helps the coach to also gain deeper understanding of the client's issues. It helps in managing and controlling the flow of conversation, especially when the clients go off the tangent.

For example:

Coach: Tell me three specific actions you accomplished from your last session with me.

Client: The week was miserable. An incident occurred in the family and... **[Off the tangent response]**

Coach: I'm sorry about what happened; if you want, we can talk about it at the end of the session. Could you tell me just three actions you performed after our session last week.

Client: Well, I reviewed the customer's file, and started my report on the case before the incident occurred, and I could no longer continue. I have not written the full report yet. **[On-Course response]**

From the above discussion, it is clear that the coach has set the pace for the session, but the communication cycle is not yet complete. Coaching conversation is complete when clients acknowledge that they have been understood. You can use a technique called repetition, paraphrasing, and summarising to achieve this.

## **Repetition, Paraphrasing, and Summarising**

Repetition, paraphrasing, and summarising are powerful tools used in acknowledging or validating client's thoughts and ideas. Coaches use them also to check their understanding of client's points of view.

The process involves repeating what the client said, and asking them to acknowledge whether what they repeated was exactly what they meant.

In paraphrasing, coaches substitute client's statements with their own words or phrases. This is done in order to check coach's personal understanding of the point the clients are making. They could be used also, if the coaches believe that the substituted words or phrases have better expression of client's ideas.

Continuing from our previous example, here is a demonstration of how repetition, paraphrasing and summarising can be used in coaching:

Coach: Let me confirm my understanding of what you just said. So regardless of the incident that occurred, you were able to carry out full research on the customer. What is remaining for you to complete is writing a report about the customer. Is that correct? **[ Coach seeking acknowledgment]**

Client: Absolutely! And I believe I should be able to combine it with any action plans I will get from today's session. **[Client acknowledges]**

Summarising opens up new insights for clients, while verbatim repetition creates the impression in the client's minds that the coach is paying attention, and gaining understanding in their conversation.

## **Pauses and Silence**

In coaching, SILENCE is golden.

Coaches use silence as a tool to give opportunity to clients to reflect, and think before providing answer to questions.

Silence can be intimidating to new coaches because they find it hard to understand why they should simply shut their mouth, and wait for their clients to reflect or thing through their responses, sometimes for a long time. So the tendency for them is to quickly jump in with different question that could divert the clients thought pattern.

Coaching conversation involves deep thinking, and clients need a lot of time to process their thoughts before answering them. It is good practice for coaches to allow sufficient time between questions, so clients can think before answering.

Sometimes though, silence could become a sign that the client is stuck, and need support. So while waiting for clients to process and respond to your question, it will be great to pay attention to their body languages to see whether they are reflecting or just stuck. If they are concentrating and making lots of eye contact, they are reflecting. But if they are looking blank, distracted or confused; they are probably stuck. If the later case is true, you may have to repeat, paraphrase, or summarise your earlier question.

# Part II
# Practicalities of Coaching

# Chapter 6

# Effective Questioning Tool

Questions are the most powerful, and frequently used of all coaching tools. They are the arsenals that set the pace for gaining clarity, raising awareness, and inducing responsibility for clients to commit to action and achieve their goals.

In this Chapter, we are going to consider what constitutes effective questioning techniques, and how you can use them to help your clients make progress in their lives. I will also show you some of the questions to avoid, and give you reasons for avoiding them.

You need to bear in mind that not all questions produce great coaching results. So your ability to master the art of asking superior questions effectively, many of which you will find in this book, will no doubt put you in the league of experienced coaches over a short period of time, if you do not quit.

The purpose of asking questions in a coaching session is to raise curiosity in the mind of the individual, and help him or her to think at deeper level. A simple but powerful coaching question could reduce client's challenges to nothing; and open up new possibilities for them to take responsibility for creating new and better results.

However, not all questions are useful in coaching. The most effective coaching questions are **W-Questions**: What, Who, Where and When; and **H-Questions:** How or How much. W-Questions are useful for raising awareness, while **H-Questions** can be used to quantify estimates or price.

## Types of Coaching Questions

There are four types of questions which we will consider here. They are:

1. Leading questions
2. Closed questions
3. Why questions
4. Open question

## 1. LEADING Questions

Leading questions are manipulative. They have expected answers already hidden in them. People who ask leading questions knew the type of response they're expecting from their audience.

Examples of Leading Questions:

- ❖ Don't you think we should be leaving now?
- ❖ Have you thought about investing in stock X?
- ❖ What about using formula XYZ for the project?

When used in coaching, leading questions could mislead clients to believe that the answers, suggestions or ideas that follow the questions are best for them. It makes them less likely to think for themselves make their own choices, and find their own solutions.

It is highly recommended for coaches not to ask leading questions in their coaching. But if clients run out of ideas (as they sometimes do) and asks for coach's opinion, idea or suggestion in a matter, it is good practice to offer some, if the coach has one.

Notwithstanding, coaches must make their clients aware that by no means should they consider suggestions from the coach more superior to those generated by them. Instead, they should encourage them to weigh importance of the suggestions in relation to the issues being discussed, and accept or reject them.

## 2. **CLOSED Question**

A closed question elicits a simple 'Yes' or 'No' response. Closed questions are not useful in all coaching sessions because they tend to shut the door to further questioning. However, closed questions can be useful for reaching agreement on action plans, or confirmation of details.

For example:

> Coach: Are you committed to completing these actions within two weeks as you said earlier?

In order to maximise coaching results, it is highly recommended to avoid closed questions. The purpose of questioning is to engage clients in conversations, where they are able to think deeply through their situations, and find answers to the challenges they are facing. Closed questions are not designed to fulfill this objective. Closed questions begin with "Do, Have, Has, Is or Are," and have the propensity of limiting coaching conversations.

Below are some examples of a closed question that need not be used in coaching:

- Have you learned anything from this exercise?
- Do you have a strategy for solving this problem?
- Are there barriers in your way that are stopping you?
- Are these the only choices you can think of?
- Has this coaching session helped you in any way?

## 3. WHY Questions (WQ)

Why questions are not usually powerful and results-focused for coaching purposes.

Why questions evoke defensive responses from the person asked. Take for example someone says:

*"Why did you do that?"*

The usual initial thought in the minds of the person to whom the question was asked could be: I'm criticized, disapproved, or judged. A 'Why' question makes people to give lots of excuses, and creates wrong assumptions in an attempt for them to justify their actions.

Since coaching conversations are intended to be non-judgmental and make clients not feel criticized, coaches need to exercise caution when using 'Why' questions. Although, a question such as; *Why does this matter to you?* could be asked occasionally if your 'What' questions does not reveal enough information.

## 4. OPEN Questions

Open questions are great for coaching. They are predominantly used in coaching because of their potency for helping clients to look at the bigger picture.

Open questions are non-judgmental, and encourage creative thinking. It helps clients to explore their own ideas without pressure from any external force. Open questions begin with *What, Who, Where* and *When*.

For example:

Coach: What plans do you have for reaching your deadline tomorrow?

Notice that the question sounds safe and unthreatening. Unlike a closed question, you cannot answer an open question with a simple **'Yes'** or **'No'** answer.

## Turning 'Closed' Questions to 'OPEN' Questions

Below are examples of how you can turn 'Closed Questions' (CQ) to 'Open Questions' (OQ).

i) CQ: Do you have enough strength to complete this task?

OQ: What strengths do you have to help you accomplish this task? You could also say: When have you used your strengths in a similar task previously?

ii) CQ: Has this session helped you?

OQ: How has this session helped you? What have you learned from this session? Or, What difference has this session made to you?

These questions help clients to identify any progress they have made from learning.

iii) CQ: Are there any barriers stopping your progress?
OQ: What barriers are in your way? What has to happen for you to proceed?

iv) CQ: Is that OK?

OQ: How do you feel about that? What's your response to that?

These questions help clients examine their thoughts and feelings.

v) CQ: Is that all?

OQ: What more can you tell me?

This encourages your client to dig deeper.


vi) CQ: Does this happen all the time?

OQ: When does this happen? Where does this happen?
Clients can be more descriptive with these types of questions.

## Exploring OPEN Questions

Since coaching conversations are predominantly based on Open Questioning Techniques, I'd like to go a little deeper in this section, to explore the subsets of open questions, how they are used, and when you can use them.

First of all, let us consider Open Questions in the following three contexts:

A. Questioning for clarity,
B. Questions that follow interest, and
C. Challenging questions.

## A. Questioning for Clarity

When clients need clarity or deeper understanding on an issue; the ideal types of questions to ask are W-Questions. They begin with "what, Who, Where and When," and can be used in getting clients to think, as well as clarify understanding of words or phrases used by them.

For example:

> Coach: What specifically do you mean by...?

W-Question questions can be useful in two ways. First, in clarifying *pronouns* – he, she, or they, used by the client; or in qualifying a person or thing that the coach is not clear about.

For example:

> Client: He asked him to leave his office.
>
> Coach: Tell me, who specifically said that, and to whom?

Another way 'W-Questions' can be used is to obtain complete list of people or things involved in a matter.

For example:

Coach: 'Who' or 'What' else is involved in the matter?" Or Who are the other members on the team?

Questions that begin with 'Where' and 'When' can be asked to find specific locations in time and place.

For example:

Client: I can't make any headway with this report.

Coach: Where exactly in the report are you not able to make headway?

Client: I read the report to the end, but I can't find any conclusion he has made.

In a typical coaching situation, this type of question could lead to the following dialogue:

Coach: So what can you do now?

Client: I will speak to my manager about it for clarification.

Coach:   When exactly will you do that?

Client:   Today; immediately after lunch.

'How' questions are useful for connecting a verb (a 'doing word') in order to gain high quality information very quickly. How much adds clarity and raises awareness when issues relating to quantity, size or scale are discussed. This can be demonstrated in the following ways:

Client:   I am certain we've exceeded our budget on training.

Coach:   Tell me; by how much?

Client:   10%. (Or he may choose to state it in absolute terms and say $10,000).

Another version of a 'How Much' question, which potentially raises awareness, is demonstrated below:

Client:   You know; I'm worried that the strategy introduced by George last week might not work.

Coach:   By how much on a scale of 1 to 10 are you worried?

Client:     About 4 or 5.

Coach:    So do you want us to discuss it now?

Client:     Absolutely not, I think we can go ahead and discuss the program for tomorrow's meeting.

Clarifying questions can be daunting sometimes. Nevertheless, with constant practicing, you will get used to asking them. They are useful for coaches to avoid making the mistake of unnecessary assumptions on a subject matter.

## B. Questions that follow interest

As I said earlier, questions that follow client's interest validate their thoughts and ideas. They demonstrate coach's attentiveness to client's discussion. They also demonstrates how curious a coach is in learning more about their client's subject matter.

A statements or question that follow interest can be asked to follow-up an existing conversation. It could be something as:

*"Really? Tell me more about that"*, or
*"You said you'd like to consider a number of options, could you tell me about it?"*

## C. Challenging Questions

Let's examine this scenario:

Suppose I was coaching Andrew, who had responsibility for producing his departmental budget, which was meant to be included in the company's annual master budget. The budget will be due for presentation to the board three weeks from today. However, up till now, Andrew does not seem to have any clear direction about his department's targets, and couldn't just make them up.

I asked Andrew to tell me how he could get the information he needed to build up the budget within the remaining time before the board meeting; he said he could speak to his line-manager about it.

Then I asked him to tell me when he might do that and he went blank...

Few minutes passed, and I repeated the same question and he said: "I don't know if I'd like to go to him for this."

What could be your reason? I asked. "I'm just thinking of leaving the company," he replied. When are you leaving? He said: "I'm not even sure yet."

From this conversation, it became clear that Andrew held some beliefs that were sabotaging his ability to go on with his work. So I challenged his belief and said:

> *"Andrew, if you don't get clear direction about your department's budget from your line-manager, you would ultimately not complete this task to deadline, unless you are prepared to produce some sub-optimal numbers. Nevertheless, you could fall in to the risk of facing a disciplinary action, or losing your job. Please tell me; when are you going to discuss this with your line-manager?"*

Here's the thing; sometimes, your clients may exhibit beliefs that limit their chances of making progress with their goals or work.

As a good coach, you need to be courageous, and challenge such disempowering beliefs to get them moving toward again toward their goals. Negative believes could take different forms and include the following:

- ❖ I always get things wrong.
- ❖ I can't speak in public.
- ❖ It doesn't work.
- ❖ I've tried it before.
- ❖ I'm pretty sure he doesn't like me.

The problem with negative beliefs is that clients hold them as true without proof; and the beliefs stop them from taking the actions they should take towards reaching their goals.

By challenging and exposing clients limiting beliefs, coaches are invariably unstucking them from set back, and clearing their pathway for progress.

Here are more examples:

Coach: I believe you're enjoying your work in this organisation.

Client: Not true, the people here are very unfriendly.

Coach: What makes you say so? **[Challenging question]**

Client: Well, nobody talks to me here.

Coach: Really! Nobody?

Client: Well only a few.

Coach: Who are the few?

Client: My manager and some other colleagues.

Coach: How many people need to talk to you, for you to feel the place is friendly? **[Challenging question]**

Client: At least more than that.

Coach: Precisely how many?

Client: Everyone.

Coach: How realistic is it for everyone in the organisation to be friendly with you? **[Challenging question]**

Client: Eh…m; I think it's not realistic really.

Sometimes, clients fail to take action to reach their goals. This could be caused genuinely by work interruptions

Notwithstanding, if interruptions become regular and the clients are constantly falling behind deadlines, you can challenge them with the following examples of challenging questions:

- ❖ What is holding you from achieving your goal?

- ❖ How important are these goals to you right now?

- ❖ What needs to happen for you to take responsibility for achieving your goal?

- ❖ By how much is this inaction affecting you everyday?

# Chapter 7

# GROW Model

As leaders of various businesses and organisations, one of your most crucial roles is ensuring that your support team have the skills and ability to deliver their best performance in any given situation. This helps the individuals to make informed decisions, develop new skills, solve problems and contribute enormously to the growth of the business as well as their own personal career development.

Many successful leaders measure their successes on the basis of their team's rate of development and growth. Unfortunately, many leaders do not have the formal training to coach their teams to develop, grow and succeed.

To some the sound of coaching is overwhelming; and they wonder where and how to begin. But the good news is that there are lots of tools and techniques available in coaching to help you become a good coach.

One of those tools is the GROW Model.

GROW Model is a powerful framework for organising successful coaching sessions. It versatile and can be applied to any area of coaching. GROW provides structure for coaching conversations in ways that produce powerful and meaningful results to clients.

The word GROW is derived from the first letters of each stage in the GROW model process; in other words, GROW is a mnemonic. The model is not a theory or principle, but a standard that grew out of 'best practices,' which was developed in 1980s by Sir John Whitmore and highly recommended for all coaches.

GROW stands for the following:

**G:** Goal
**R:** Reality
**O:** Options
**W:** Will or Way Forward


As I already said, the GROW model is highly recommended for planning the structure of coaching sessions. It begins first by determining where the client wants to go (**goal**). Then it considers their current situations (**reality**), obstacles in the way (**Options**) and the commitments they have to make to overcome the obstacles (**Will or Way Forward)** in order to reach their destinations. GROW model is the crux of coaching and forms an important Chapter of this book.

## Goal Setting (G)

The golden rule is that your client brings to coaching, the goal he or she wants to achieve. It must be something of value and importance to them; for example a new house, a car, a new job, starting a business. Someone's goal can also be to change some behaviours that no longer serve them.

It is the responsibility of the client to bring or introduce the goal. Even in workplace, where managers initiate sessions to resolve specific employee's issue, it is appropriate for the employee (client) to be given the benefit of determining the goal for the session.

Goal setting is an important stage in the entire GROW process. It aims to identify, clarify, and agree a number of key specific, realistic, and measurable outcomes, which are essential to the client.

By asking useful questions such as:

- What has brought you to coaching?
- What would you like to get out of this half an hour we'll spend together?
- What would be a good outcome for you from this session today?

A dialogue might ensue in which your clients could answer as follows:

- An action plan to write up my budget for the year.
- An outline for the month that I can adopt.
- How to identify key decisions in my next meeting with management.
- An plan towards getting my next promotion.
- To get my team to take responsibility.

It is important for coaches to gain clarity about the goals their clients bring to coaching, and be able to clearly distinguish them between **end** goal and **performance** goal.

An **end goal** is the ultimate outcome the client seeks to achieve. The house, car, or change in behaviour. It could also be 'promotion' as well as 'team taking ownership of their work.' In sports, a client's goal could be: "To win the Gold Medal in the next Olympic Games, or World Cup." In many instances, end goals are audacious and usually out of the control of coaches and clients to achieve.

**Performance goals** are the series of daily, weekly or monthly tasks, which clients are committed to take to reach their end goals. They consist of simple action steps agreed to be taken by clients during the coaching sessions. These goals are under the control of clients.

## Qualities of A Good Goal

A good coach must ensure that his or her client's goal is not only **S M A R T**:

- ❖ **S**pecific
- ❖ **M**easurable
- ❖ **A**greed
- ❖ **R**ealistic
- ❖ **T**ime phased

But

**P U R E:**

- ❖ Positively stated
- ❖ Understood
- ❖ Relevant
- ❖ Ethical

And

**C L E A R:**

- ❖ Challenging
- ❖ Legal
- ❖ Environmentally sound
- ❖ Appropriate
- ❖ Recorded

The idea behind identifying the qualities of a good goal is to provide an appropriate basis for measuring all goals. For example, the guiding principle is that goals must be congruent with values in order to be achieved. Notwithstanding, if goals are not **realistic**, they lack the hope for achieving, and if they're not **challenging** enough, they become less inspiring to pursue.

A good goal needs to be stated in **positive** present tense. For example, "I am reaching half-a-million Dollar sales target by the end of June;" instead of: "I don't want to sell less than half-a-million Dollar by the end of June." Negative goals – (lese than half-a-million Dollar sale) drives individual's energy and attention negatively.

Goals must be **agreed** between the parties setting them. Agreement must also be extended to the teams, who will be involved in executing the tasks. Where there is no agreement between the manager and team executing the goals or project, people seldom take responsibility, and performance and results suffer.

It's important to point out also that goals need to be **legal, ethical and environmentally** sound. A goal that aims to contradict the law, or put society in disadvantage, lacks integrity.

## Sample Coaching Session on GOAL

Here is sample coaching session that demonstrates how coach can coach their clients to establish a good goal:

Coach: It's really nice having this conversation with you today. What would you like to take home from the 60 minutes we'll spend together?

Client: Well, I'd like to get some strategies to finish my work on deadline.

Coach: Do you mean strategies for the rest of your career life or what?

Client: Oh no; that would be just too much for now. I'm looking for a realistic plan of action, which I can commit to within the next three or five months?

Coach: Great, so how many months in particular are we going to be considering?

Client: I think three months will be just fine.

| | |
|---|---|
| Coach: | Tell me; what would finishing your work to deadline mean to you? |
| Client: | I feel guilty and sometimes loss of confidence because I turn my reports in late every time. I really want to regain my confidence and get more inspired. |
| Coach: | How would you know if you turn your report in to deadline, regain your confidence and get more inspired? |
| Client: | Oh, if I hand my report to my manager on the 5th day of the new month, that would be a confirmation to me. That would also boost my confidence to motivate others to do the same. |
| Coach: | So by what day and month do you want to see yourself actually meeting this deadline? |
| Client: | By the end of the third month. |
| Coach: | That sounds good; what day and month specifically do you want it by? |
| Client: | 30th April. |

## Checking for REALITY (R)

**Reality** stage of the GROW model is where client's goals are subjected to intense clarity-check; bringing it into sharper focus to re-enforce, modify or drop it.

In the 'Reality' stage, the coach assists the client to objectively assess where they currently are in relation to their goal, and how they feel about their current situation. This is a discovery process that helps them to gain vivid clarity about the goal, understand what drives their emotions for the goal, and identify any concerns or dissatisfactions they currently entertain.

Sometimes, people try to solve their problems without truly giving adequate considerations to their starting point. They seem to confront their issues and often miss critical amount of input that would help them make better decisions.

The primary objective of a 'Reality' stage of the GROW Model is not for the coach to solve the problem, make suggestions, or draw a conclusion. Instead, it is to gain more understanding of the situations of the client in relation to the goal. It happens that as the coach gains more understanding on the issue, and the client becomes more aware of his or her own circumstances, both parties eventually get to a position where, the coach asks more powerful questions, and the client makes better choices.

In a typical coaching situation, reality-check lays emphasis on facts and figures; events that took place, actions that were taken, challenges in the way of the client, and resources they need to achieve the goal. To make the client think deeper, 'W-Questions, 'What,' 'Who,' 'Where' and 'When;' as well as 'How Much' questions are usually asked.

Continuing from our last conversation on goal:

Coach: Let's take a look at the way things are right now. You mentioned that "you turn-in your reports late every time; how many reports did you turn in late in the past three months?

Client: About two, and my line-manager wasn't happy about it.

Coach: Can you tell me more about it?

Client: I was required to produce monthly activity report of my department.

The report involves giving account of projects and tasks handled by my team during the month. It was meant to be ready by the end of the first week of the new month, but I have been submitting mine in the second week. This is becoming embarrassing to my team and me.

Coach: How embarrassing is this becoming to you and your team?

Client: Well, I guess we're being perceived as ineffective, which I think might put us in the 'bad books.'

Coach: What is your line-manager saying about this?

Client: He feels frustrated about it too. At one time, he said management thinks we're wasting too much time in our work.

Coach: What else is not working as they should in your department?

Client: I noticed that the quality of work of my team members is diminishing. They are making serious mistakes than before. I guess they too have lost confidence.

Coach: So far in this conversation, you have mentioned about your inability to meet deadline, lack of personal and team confidence, your line-manager's frustration, and the view of management about your department. What else have you not told me?

Client: I can't think of anything else right now.

Coach: Okay, which of the four issues would you like us to focus on first in this session?

Client: The bit about meeting deadlines. That's the biggest one.

## **Exploring Possible OPTIONS (O)**

Options is the stage, where the coach helps his or her clients to determine what is possible for reaching their objectives. It is a brainstorming stage that give opportunity for clients to generate as many alternative courses of actions as possible, before deciding on the best ones to choose.

These list of actions are believed to potentially take them to their end goals, if implemented.

As coaches, we let them do most of the talking without offering any suggestions or making decisions for them. We maintain a disposition that gives them confidence and safety to express their ideas and thoughts without resistance or fear of being judged by us. This creates trust and helps in sharing their pains.

Sometimes, client's reality can be curtailed by their own limiting beliefs about how they expect the world to be. These beliefs often lead them to make wrong assumptions that hold them back from making progress.

For example; a client could say things like:

- ❖ It cannot work.
- ❖ We can't afford the time.
- ❖ I'm too old.
- ❖ That's not how we do it here.
- ❖ He just hates me.

Let us continue our coaching conversation on GROW model, and take our clients through the Options stage.

| | |
|---|---|
| Coach: | Now, what are the different things you could do, to be able to meet your next reporting deadline at the end of this month? |
| Client: | I could write up with a plan of things to do early enough before the month ends. |
| Coach: | Okay, so tell me the first thing you could start doing early enough before the month ends. |
| Client: | My department receives input from Administrations team to compile our report every month. I could request them to send their input one week earlier. |
| Coach: | What else could you do? |
| Client: | I could speak with the Head of Information Technology to produce end-of-the-month report for my department on the last day of the month, instead of waiting for the 3$^{rd}$ of the new month. |
| Coach: | What other things can you think of? |

Client: If I could let my team start developing contents of the reports by the 28th of every month, would that help?

Coach: Well, I suppose that's a great one, what do you think?

Client: I think so!

Coach: Fantastic! Tell me; what else could you do?

Client: Oh! I could now share the tasks among my team members, so everyone becomes aware of his or her own responsibility towards month-end reporting for our department.

Coach: That sounds great!

Let us look at the list of options you have generated so far. You said that you could:

- ❖ Make a plan of things to do early before the month ends.
- ❖ Request Administrations department to send their input one week earlier.

- ❖ Speak with Head of IT to generate month-end-report for you on the last day of every month for you.
- ❖ Delegate month-end responsibilities to your team members, and ask them to develop their contents by the 28th day of every month.

Coach: What other things could you do that you have not yet mentioned?

Client: I can't think of any other thing for now.

## Deciding the WILL or WAY FORWARD

The 'Will' or 'Way Forward' section of GROW Model is where ideas are turned into decisions from the list of possible Options already generated. It is the stage where clients make commitment to take specific actions that would move them forward towards their goal.

By asking useful questions, the client establishes his 'will' and motivation to engage in careful execution of plans that would take them one step to the goal.

Below is a list of possible useful questions you can ask at the 'Options' stage:

- ❖ Which of these options are your going to start with first?
- ❖ What are you going to do now?
- ❖ When are you going to do it?
- ❖ Will this action meet your goal?
- ❖ What obstacles might you meet along the way?
- ❖ Who needs to know?
- ❖ What support do you need to do this?
- ❖ How and when are you going to get that support?
- ❖ What other considerations do you have?
- ❖ On a scale of 1 to 10, how certain are you to carrying out these tasks?
- ❖ What prevents it from being a 7?
- ❖ What can you do to stay motivated?
- ❖ What could potentially stop you from taking these actions?

In continuation of our example coaching conversation, here is the conclusion how the coach works the client through the Options Stage:

Coach: Looking at the list of five options you already have, what are you going to do now?

Client: I think the most important one for me to begin with is speaking with the Administrations team leader to ensure we receive their input by the 28th of every month.

Coach: When are you going to speak to him?

Client: Today is Thursday; I will speak to him on Monday, next week.

Coach: What time do you consider suitable for speaking with him?

Client: Oh, 09:30a.m will be suitable before he heads off to other meetings.

Coach: What else are you going to do next?

Client: I will meet with the Head of IT on the same day, but at 3:00p.m.

Coach: What else?

Client: I will hold a meeting with my team tomorrow morning to discuss the plan of action, and make them aware of their respective involvement in the new plan.

**Coach:** What do you think might be the appropriate time for this meeting with your team?

**Client:** First thing tomorrow. I think 09:00a.m would be ideal.

**Coach:** It seems you have allocated all five options into your plan of action. What in your opinion have we not yet considered to include in this?

**Client:** I just realized that I have not included my line-manager's involvement in the plan.

**Coach:** You are correct. What would you like to include him for?

**Client:** I guess it would be appropriate for him to be aware of the plan, and if there's any suggestions or support we could get from him, that could help.

**Coach:** Well I think so too, but how are you going to make him aware of this?

**Client:** I could hold a meeting with him.

Coach: Is this something you could do, or something you know that you will do?

Client: Oh, it's something I will do! I will meet with him tomorrow, immediately after meeting with my team to share the plan with him, and seek his suggestions. I will do this by 10:30a.m.

Coach: You are certainly making progress! What else can you do?

Client: Eh...mm, I think we've covered everything.

Coach: If you put these six items on a scale of 1 to 10, how certain are you that they will help you meet this month's deadline?

Client: I'm already getting excited about this month's deadline. It's going to be an 8+.

Coach: Great! What could you do to make it a 9?

Client: Actually, I think it is a 10!

Coach: Fantastic! Who do you need to share this plan with, that could hold you accountable?

Client: As I said, I will share with my line-manager and team members.

Coach: That's fine. What do you think might get in the way of holding the meeting with your team and line-manager tomorrow?

Client: Nothing I can think of now.

## Summary of the GROW Model

As I have said several times in this book, the objective of any coaching session is to help the client gain clarity of what he or she wants, just as they want it.

By taking clients through the 'Reality' stage, you are able to raise their **awareness** about where they are presently, in relation to where they want to be. You also help them understand the circumstances that are responsible for being where they are. 'Reality' opens up the bigger picture of their past and present conditions, and helps them to see what's missing in reaching where they're going.

'Options' is a brainstorming stage that allows clients to think creatively about what is possible for them to do, in order to move one step forward towards their goals. The effectiveness of the 'Options' stage depends on a *clearly defined* 'Goal,' and very importantly also, a thoroughly explored 'Reality' about client's situation. Unless these two GROW model stages are properly dealt with, clients may get stuck or run out of creativity abut what they can do to move forward at the Options stge.

The 'Will or Way Forward' stage is the commitment stage. I can be said to be the point, where the robber meets the road.

As we know, achievement of goals depend largely on execution of carefully selected plan of actions that are important to the goal. The 'Will' stage of GROW has the coach supporting clients to make commitment with their time, money, and other resources, towards choosing and executing what has been agreed.

The entire process can be stretching sometimes; but the results can be overwhelmingly phenomenal compared to someone working alone.

Overall, the coach plays the role of an accountability partner for the purpose of ensuring that the client achieves their goals.

# Chapter 8

# Coaching For High Performance

There is misconception about the term high performance people. To many, it refers only to individuals with extraordinary talents to perform in the military or game of sports.

But in the context of this book, coaching for high performance is the process of supporting individuals of every age, sex, or background, with proven tools and techniques to improve their work and produce greater results.

In a workplace situation, it can be useful in turning an entire organisation into a high performance environment, where managers, leaders, and employees collaborate seamlessly to produce extra-ordinary results constantly.

The starting point for achieving high performance results through coaching begins with aligning client's (employee's) goals, roles or activities with their respective values; and exploring their 'realities' to ensure they are in sync with their objectives..

It is essential to develop crystal clear vision that vividly defines the directions that high performance individuals are headed. The essence is to constantly explore their motivation, and overcome any obstacles that might hold them back in the process.

High performance coaching involves challenging clients, as well as providing support for them to stay focused. The tool is particularly useful for achieving crucial long-term goals, going through a fundamental change process, or overcoming major setback in career, business or life. Unlike coaching as it were, it involves taking more direct approach with clients and employees to ensure they reach and maintain their high performance levels.

In order to achieve successful high performance coaching results, coaches are required to:

- ❖ Respect the individuals being coached
- ❖ Pay attention to their skills and goals
- ❖ Provide honest constructive feedback and challenge where necessary.
- ❖ Mind your state, and not allow your personal ego and agenda get in the way.
- ❖ Be conversant with the application of useful coaching tools and techniques for achieving desired high performance results, one of which is *Performance |Gap| Result* in the diagram below.

When working with high performance teams, it is possible for managers and coaches to determine the direction their employees or clients are headed by first defining a clear vision for them. Particularly in a workplace situation, managers can develop vision statements that clearly states what the future looks like for the employees or team, and how to know when they reach there. To be congruent, departmental vision needs to align with the overall company's vision statement.

In coaching corporate executives, I've been asked severally by managers to explain why they should go through the rigour of developing visions statements, when it is the responsibility of senior management to do so.

Great question!

In a typical organisation, it is the responsibility of senior management to define the mission, vision and values (MVV) of the organisation and continuously communicate it to the entire workforce.

As you are aware, mission tells the people what the organisation is set up for – *the purpose factor*. Vision speaks about where the organisation is going and where they want to be when it grows up, say 20 years from now – *the direction factor*. And values are the written codes and uncompromising conduct, behaviour and attitude, which are expected of the people within and outside the organisation as they all work together to reach the organisation's vision – *the attitudinal factor*.

Having understood the meaning of these terms,, it is needful for departmental managers or divisional heads to make clear statements about the direction they are leading their departments and teams in their effort towards achieving the corporate vision. Ultimately, the objective of departmental vision should not be different from the organisation's corporate vision, but it should clarify, and break down the department's responsibility in the overall vision.

Coaching for high performance is only effective after the clients or employees have gained vivid understanding of what they're aiming for; and the motivation behind their actions. This can be achieved by coaching, in combination with GROW model.

Performance is directly linked with potential. In my opinion, high performance occurs by setting the highest standards of expectation, and tapping into client's strengths and potential to deliver the result, which sometimes exceeds expectation.,

But in many instances, people's potentials are grossly under-utilized because of the *gap* between potential and performance, which leads to low performance.

In other words, people's ability to unleash their full potential and reach their star performance can be sabotaged by what I refer to as *the gap*.

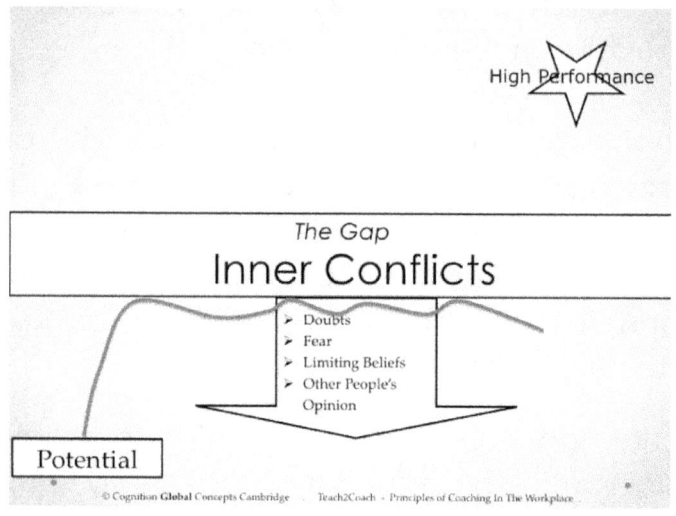

Performance Gap.
Designed by Nkem Paul for Cognition Global Concepts

**Potential**   | *The Gap* |   **Performance**

The fundamental factors that sabotage peak performance in many individuals I've come across, are mostly the inhabitants of *The Gap*. In Chapter One, I referred to them as *Inner*

*Conflicts.*

Inner conflicts take different forms and shapes, and include fear of failure or loss of confidence; guilt, trying too hard, worry, aiming for 100% (perfection), other people's opinions, as well as disempowering beliefs. Each element of inner conflict is responsible for widening the gap between people's potential and their highest performance.

In order to achieve star performance consistently, coaches need to support their clients to eliminate the presence of inner conflicts, with a view to ultimately close the gap. The can be achieved by focusing on three key outcomes:

1. Set a clear vision and goal,
2. Eliminate inner conflicts,
3. Motivate and inspire to maximise potential.

Successful high performance managers, leaders, athletes, and professionals in every field of work overcome the limitations imposed by inner conflicts, create clear compelling visions and goals and achieve extraordinary results by embracing high performance coaching.

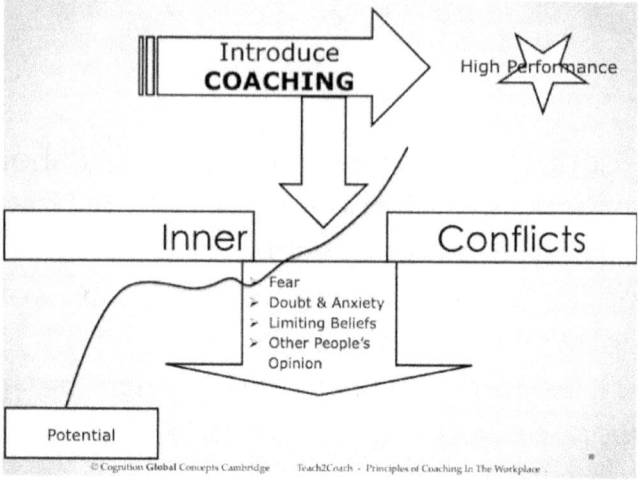

Performance Gap.
Designed by Nkem Paul for Cognition Global Concepts

# How to Create Star Performance

## 1. Create clear compelling vision and goals

Without vision and goal, people drift. As I explained in previous pages, vision talks about a future destination, which people are excited about reaching. It is the internal image we paint, of where we want to be. A clear compelling vision give rise to audacious goals; goals that stretch our capabilities (potentials) but are achievable.

Goals that lead to high performance results are usually scary; but their usefulness to the individual's existence makes them inspiring to pursue.

Successful athletes, entrepreneurs and other high achievers set great goals that stretch, motivate, as well as boost their self-confidence to pursue and achieve them.

It is often said that if you don't know where you are going, everywhere looks the same. In line with that statement, clearly defined vision eliminates disagreement, argument or ambiguity about the direction to follow, or the confusion about how to identify the destination when clients reaches there. In terms of goals, it clearly states the "What" that the client is seeking to achieve.

Let us examine a conversation between a coach and his staff Kate, who needed to be supported to get back to her high performance form:

COACH: *After my meeting with the Director of Finance this morning, it was obvious that the last monthly report was submitted late. He mentioned also, that the usual in-depth and succinct analysis of costs, profitability and trends, which he enjoys reading were full of mistakes and frowned that the department's excellent performance is gradually disappearing.*

*The aim of my discussion with you now is to identify specific goals and breakthrough measures you can implement to mitigate further lateness and errors in your report, and more importantly get back into your high performance position.*

*What might be the most helpful thing for you to take away from this discussion?*

As you can see, the coach has carefully articulated the specific issues at hand to Kate, who is responsible for producing the department's monthly financial reports. He concluded by asking Kate to identify one key goal she could work on from their session.

It is not always compulsory for the introduction to be as elaborate as above. In practice, it is advisable to explain the situation to the client (employee) to avoid concealment of any important information. Also, communicating the situation without bias and in a way that makes the client feel safe, promotes trust and employee-manager relationship. In response, Kate says...

CLIENT: If I'm honest with you, the most important thing I'd like to talk about in this respect is the unsupportive attitude of my colleagues towards me, especially at month end.

COACH: What nature of unsupportive attitude does your colleagues put up towards you at month-ends?

CLIENT: Well, in the past three consecutive months, information for writing up the report, which normally comes to me two to three days before deadline, has been getting to me on the last day of submission of report. This puts me under serious pressure.

COACH: So your colleagues have been turning in their reports only on the day it was meant for submission to the FD; is that what you mean?

CLIENT: Exactly!

COACH: I see. Bearing in mind that we have only 45 minutes remaining to end this discussion, what one thing would you like to take home towards remedying this situation?

CLIENT: Okay; I'd like to get my colleagues to submit their reports early enough to me.

COACH: What exactly do you mean when you say early enough?

CLIENT: 3 days to my submission deadline. That would be on the 28$^{th}$ day of every month.

COACH: How will achieving this goal change your performance?

CLIENT: I need minimum of three days to consolidate my financial report, get it reviewed with my manager, and

|  | make any suggested update before it goes to management. I believe three days is a good period for me to be in good control of this. |
|---|---|
| COACH: | That sounds good to me. What would be happening for you to know that these reports have actually been submitted to you on the due date? |
| CLIENT: | At least the reports would have been put in my month-end file, ready for use. |
| COACH: | Could I ask you to write this goal down in your diary, just as you have said it to me? I will also do the same. |

By setting a clear goal for receiving month-end related input on or before the 28th day of every month, Kate has clearly identified what she considers a major step towards returning to high star performance position.

## 2. Eliminate inner conflicts

Inner conflicts are a combination of factors such as fear, doubts, anxiety, guilt, or limiting beliefs that stand in the way of a person's performance.

By nature, human beings have tendency to create their own limitations. These limitations occur as a result of perceptions and beliefs they accept to be true, which distort their focus, and divert attention from their reality.

Take for instance, in corporate organisations and other professional settings; people perform roles or study courses that automatically become their identity. This is common among accountants, lawyers, doctors, teachers and many others in different professions.

When people are identified by what they do or studied, they almost develop tough predisposition for it, as if that was the only skills they have potential for in reality. When they are assigned other roles, they engage in all manner of defensive behaviour to absolve themselves from taking up the new roles. Their attitude towards other roles makes it seem as if the only role they can perform is accountancy, or law.

The second types of limitations that get in people's way of reaching their potentials are self-imposed limiting beliefs, and inner conflict that resides in the gap.

Below is typical example of *inner conflict* in operation and how coaching can be used to eliminate it.

Clare is the head of Banking Operations in one of the popular high street banks in Cambridge. I'm not sure about the course Clare studied at college, but it definitely was not finance because when it comes to preparing budget, Clare tells me: "I can't prepare budget because I'm not a finance person." Although there is no truth to validate Clare's phobia for budgeting, the fact remains that she cannot prepare one, no matter how much she try until she eliminates her beliefs about finance and budget.

In helping Clare overcome her limitation, the following coaching conversation ensued:

COACH: Clare, you remember mentioning to me that you couldn't prepare a budget because you're not a finance person; since when did that become your reality?

CLIENT: Well, I'm not sure about when, but I guess it's true.

COACH: Yeah..., but since when did it become a universal truth?

CLIENT: I'm not sure, but I guess budget preparation is meant for finance people hence I can't do it. I'm not a finance person.

COACH: Is this just what you guess or...?

CLIENT: May be it's just my guess.

COACH: I see; so how would you think differently if you knew you could prepare a budget?

CLIENT: E eh...m ; that would be great! I'd probably give it a go.

COACH: Even as a non-finance person?

CLIENT: Yeah... I guess I could go on training just to learn how to do it.

COACH: What difference would that make to your work?

CLIENT: A lot! I would be able to prepare my branch budget by myself.

Inner conflicts present enormous obstacles to high performance. They threaten their victims with fear, self-doubt and guilt; and until they are removed, the individuals would remain imprisoned in mediocrity.

It is the responsibility of coaches to support clients to look at their issues from different perspectives. The aim is to gain new awareness about their true identities, as well as create new realities for themselves.

## 3. Motivate and inspire to maximise potential.

There are many ways to motivate people to perform effectively. One of such ways is by ensuring that the individual understands the vision of the organisation they work for, and also providing the resources they needed to work towards reaching that vision. Other than providing all tools necessary to do the job, managers need to support, encourage, and reward their staff constantly, as a means of encouraging them to use their best ability to work.

Positive motivation is by far one of the fundamental traditional management and leadership techniques for creating enthusiasm in employees to maximise performance. As you will soon learn in Chapter Nine, motivation is perhaps one of the biggest incentives used by successful managers and leaders to engage, energize, and release individual's best effort towards achieving personal and organisational goals.

As little as *"That was a brilliant performance"* said to a colleague by the manager can be; it can go a long way to boost their morale. To understand what motivates a staff, a coach can ask simple questions such as:

- ❖ What would you like to be rewarded with when you achieve this goal?
- ❖ How would you like to celebrate your success if you complete the task?
- ❖ If everything goes according to plan, how would you be feeling?
- ❖ How would you be feeling as a result of others people (or customers) succeeding from using your product or service?

The bottom line is that motivation and inspiration need to be consistent to be effective. Coaches should help their clients to see how their contributions fit in the overall scheme of things within their organisations. They need to be made to feel relevant in the success of their customers or organisation through their personal inputs no matter how small.

## Driving performance through focused attention

Paying *focused attention* is perhaps the number one factor that potentially increases human capacity to create extraordinary outcomes.

Focused attention refers to a person's ability concentrate his or her energy on a specific task, object, or activity over a sustained period of time.

People who maintain focused attention always achieve much bigger results compared to those, who switch from one idea to another. It is increasingly challenging for many people to maintain sustained focus. A great majority of people pay attention on short-term activities and goals that produce short-term motivation and much quicker results.

High performance achievers pay focused attention on goals that take several months, years, and perhaps decades to accomplish. Consider the following people for example:

- ❖ Olympic athletes,
- ❖ Professional footballers,
- ❖ Successful entrepreneurs, who double productivity and profits consistently.
- ❖ High achieving leaders including presidents of nations, CEOs of companies, and other professionals.

There are many good reasons for maintaining focused attention. First, it has been proven that performance increases when the body and mind are aligned. So it helps to constantly drive energy and resources towards the object of focus or goal to create it. It also eliminates distractions, thereby releasing the individual for learning and enjoyment to occur naturally.

As I said earlier, it can be challenging to maintain focus without having a goal that motivates one. You have to have genuine interest and desire on where you're going, or what you want to achieve in order to focus well. In my Coach training workshop, my delegates watch a short video clip of six young people playing basketball game.

The teams were divided in two groups, one wearing white and the other black. I ask my delegates to count the number of times that the white players passed the basketball to their team. The interesting thing is that as the team passes the basketball, someone dressed like gorilla passes by. In almost every situation, delegates who were genuinely focused and aligned on the game did not spot the passing gorilla.

A coach has a duty to help his or her client maintain focus on their goal, and encourage them to notice any aspect they find interesting. When they get distracted, it is important to understand where their attention went. A question as simple as: **"Where did your attention go"** could be all that is necessary to make them reflect and regain awareness.

Coaching for high performance need not focus exclusively on result. Instead coaches and managers need to inspire their clients to learn and enjoy the process, because performance cannot be sustained if it does not result in learning and enjoyment.

While learning and enjoyment are important ingredients to performance, emphasis should equally be made on the quality of learning, and the impacts on long-term rather than short-term results.

High performance coaching can lead to key benefits that make significant impact on clients and their organisations as follows.

- ❖ Achievement,
- ❖ Fulfilment, and
- ❖ En(Joy)ment.

By achievement, individuals meet their goals through consistent execution of carefully selected options, strategies and ideas. Achievement helps to increase the individual's confidence and contributes to organisation's goals and bottom-line.

Fulfilment is not always a direct function of accomplishment of goals. Instead, fulfillment results from satisfaction derived from learning and growth, which occurs in the process of executing actions and achieving goals. Both the coach, client and the client's organisation participate in the benefit of fulfillment

Finally, when people achieve high performance results, they express joy (enjoyment). This happens essentially if learning and growth are part of the performance process. If people engage in learning without achievement, they get exhausted easily. If they achieve results without learning and growing in the process, soon the whole exercise becomes uninteresting, unenjoyable and complete waste of time and effort.

## Challenging clients to perform

If individuals and organisations must participate in the fundamental benefits of coaching – achievement, fulfillment and enjoyment, they need some levels of challenging in order to take action, and motivation to perform their best.

There are several factors that stop people from taking action on agreed goals. They put off actions to later days until many of them give up. In any case, the coach can help clients through challenging questions to get back on track.

## Procrastination

In his book, 'Eat That Frog' Brian Tracy advocates for people to eat a live frog first thing each morning in order to combat procrastination and get back to work. Brian used the frog metaphor to represent people's most daring or dreadful tasks.

The idea is to confront whatever you fear in order to demystify your fright.

Until you confront your fears, you may not be able to overcome it.

So Brian recommends that if there are 2 frogs to eat; be sure to eat the uglier one first. If the frog is very ugly, don't make the mistake of staring at it for too long, just grab it and eat!

The following questions can be useful in getting clients out of procrastination:

- What are you afraid of?
- What thoughts are presently disempowering you?
- What are you prepared to sacrifice to achieve this goal?
- What are you enjoying staying the same?
- What benefits are there if you take the actions and achieve your goal?
- What other opportunities could open for you when you achieve this goal?
- What will you or other people be saying to you when you have succeeded in these actions?

## Secure commitment on time and impact

In most cases, clients desire to take action on their goals. Sadly though, majority of them fail to do so in reality. By applying appropriate coaching tools, we help clients to go beyond 'desiring to do something,' and get them to do the specific things they agreed to do.

For example.

Client: This conversation has been really useful. I will go now and take action on the ideas.

Coach: What specific area of the conversation did you find useful?

Client: Well I'm now clear about possible ideas I can explore to move forward with my project.

Coach: That's great! Tell me, what specifically are you going to do first?

Client: I will schedule a meeting with Joe to discuss the budget tomorrow.

Commitment is important for creating high performance results, so coaches need to check clients level of commitment on every action they agree to take. The following questions can be used as example:

- ❖ Where will you get support as you work on this task?
- ❖ Who else needs to know about your plans?
- ❖ What gaps are there that needs to be addressed to ensure your success?
- ❖ How will you deal with de-motivational comments from others?
- ❖ On a scale of 1-10, how committed are you to taking these actions?
- ❖ What needs to happen for that to be a 10?
- ❖ What concerns do you have about carrying out these actions successfully?
- ❖ How can you get around the concerns?
- ❖ What tells you that your actions are realistic and achievable?
- ❖ What are you planning to do to celebrate your success?

# Chapter 9
# Self-Belief And Motivation

In a traditional workplace, motivation is the act of providing the proverbial *'Carrot and Stick'* in anticipation that the carrot would make people to perform much better, and the stick serves as punitive measure.

The whole essence of providing the carrot in a workplace is to give incentive for people to get things done. If managed well, motivation helps to bring the best talents and abilities out of people. The general opinion about the workplace is that people do not perform their best potential compared to how well they could in an emergency situation.

In modern day business, people will willingly engage in activities that meet their needs and purpose. This has been demonstrated in job interviews, where candidates ask their prospective employers to tell them about training and development opportunities available in their organisation, as well as the style of management they will expect.

Research has shown that job security and quality of life have been proven as having high priority in people's list of need for work. Although some people regard money as an important source of motivation, truth is that in the absence of job security and good quality of life, great majority of people will accept lesser pay to work in organisations that offer higher security and sustainability.

For people to perform their best potential, they need to be self-motivated. Management needs to adopt a new concept that makes people believe more in themselves as opposed to traditional control and autocracy. Self-belief occurs when people are given opportunity to make choices, take responsibility, and hold themselves accountable for their outcomes. Although promotion is a good motivation; promotion without empowerment to express ones initiative is counterproductive.

In 1960, Douglas McGregor, founding faculty member of MIT's Sloan School of Management argued that behind the decisions and actions of every manager are a series of assumptions about human behaviour. He summarized these assumptions in what he referred to as Theory X which says:

❖ The average human being has an inherent dislike for work and will avoid it if he can.

❖ Because people dislike work, most people must be coerced, controlled, directed and threatened with punishment to get them put forth adequate effort towards the achievement of organisational objectives.

❖ The average human being prefers to be directed; wishes to avoid responsibility, has relatively little ambition, and wants security above all.

As an alternative to Theory X, Mr. McGregor offered a new Theory Y, which rests on the following assumptions:

❖ The expenditure of physical and mental effort in work is as natural as play or rest.

- ❖ External control and threat of punishment are not the only means for bringing about effort towards organisational objectives. People will exercise self-direction and self-control in the service of objectives to which they are committed.

- ❖ Commitment to objectives is a function of the rewards associated with their achievement.

- ❖ The average human being learns under proper conditions, not only to accept but also to seek responsibility.

- ❖ The capacity to exercise a relatively high degree of imagination, ingenuity, and creativity in the solution of organisational problems is widely, not narrowly distributed in population.

- ❖ Under the conditions of modern industrial life, the intellectual potentialities or the average human being are only partly utilized.

In line with McGregor's assumptions, the goal of management should not be to simply direct and control employee. Instead, managers need to always seek to create conditions, where people are able to take responsibility and deliver maximum performance.

Empowering people to harness self-direction and self-control in pursuit of common goals is preferable to imposing a system of control designed to force them to meet objectives they have no understanding about or share. Rewarding people for doing a good job is a far more effective way to reinforce shared commitment than punishing them for failure. Beyond rewarding people, to give responsibility is more empowering, more educating, and more guaranteed to unleash the individual's creativity and contribute their best for the benefit of all.

## Effective Ways to Motivate

Some schools of taught believe that it is not necessary to motivate people. Their argument is that motivation cannot be sustained, as factors that give rise to it such as mood, environment or events change. In my opinion, because those factors change, it even more important for managers to device more sophisticated means

To motivate their members regularly.

To understand the factors that motivate people is critical in leadership. They are the same factors that bring the best out of employees and clients, and consist mainly of:

## 1. Focus on the bigger picture.

Every organisation I have come across has a vision, mission and values statements that underpin their actions and drive their behaviour. As coach, your responsibility is to help your client or staff understand that vision and align their personal aspirations with it.

When people lose enthusiasm, passion or motivation for work, it is perhaps that they've lost the connection between 'what' they're doing, and 'why' they're doing it. 'WHY' is a critical motivational factor in performance, and people have to believe in it to make substantial progress.

If people should wake up and go to work everyday, they deserve to know how their work impacts their organisations and customers you serve.

As we studied earlier, fulfillment comes from knowing that your contribution is valuable, not only to your organisation, but also to every stakeholder involved. By deploying the right coaching tool, individuals are able to feel a sense of importance and fulfillment from their work.

## 2. Pay attention to what excites people.

The best type of motivation comes from people themselves. When having a discussion with clients or employees, pay close attention to what they say, and how they say them.

Be interested in understanding their values. Do not take this for granted if you must get the best out of them. Values can manifest in very different forms, and are often expressed in a louder, more pointed or cracked tonal voice during a conversation. You can also tell from how the person leans forward or sits upright while expressing a point.

By paying attention and understanding people's points of view, chances are they are giving you clues to what's important to them and on how best to motivate them.

## 3. Acknowledge success and praise lavishly.

Cultivate the habit of recognising and praising people anytime they complete their tasks or accomplish their goals; no matter how small.

Here's the key. If you motivate a person to take action but fail to acknowledge him when he achieves the outcome, your attitude of lack of gratitude in the project could play back negatively in their minds when you give them another task in the future.

Recognition of past successes is a great motivator for future progress and failing to acknowledge this can lead to bitterness and resentment in the mind of employees. Leading from the perspective of a coach, you are the source of constant motivation. Your team needs to come to recharge their batteries with you, and leave without feeling drained.

## 4. Apply pain and pleasure motivators.

A great way of motivating people to take action is by applying 'pain and pleasure motivators.' How many times have your read a good book and felt you should apply the author's principles? Or after attending a seminar and listening to a great speaker, how often do you go beyond being inspired or motivated to actually work on their suggestions towards improving your life or work?

I bet you seldom do; and it has nothing to do with your disobedience as people often think. The real issue is that you are not at any risk to do what they say. Your situation is neither uncomfortable nor painful enough to provoke you into action.

But let us assume that you are in danger of losing your car to your bankers for failing to pay your monthly car rental. Suppose you attended a Financial Planning seminar where the speaker gave tips on how to overcome debt challenges; would you behave differently? I bet you would take the tips very seriously and work on them.

The only reason you would work on the tips is because you are in danger of losing your car. The same is true for motivation. People's difficult times can be the catalyst that propels them to action. Stephen Covey said that satisfied needs do not motivate. It is only the unfulfilled needs that do.

## Creating motivational discomfort

How can you motivate someone who sets a goal but has consistently failed to take action? One of the ways is to apply pain and pleasure motivators.

As coach, you can put your client on a 'rocking chair' and paint two compelling images of, say three to five years into the future. The first image portrays a future characterized by worsening problems and challenges, which your client is facing now. The second image is the reverse of the first, which is a bright compelling future with everything as your client expect.

The idea is to get the client to imagine what the future holds for them three or five years from today if they fail to take action. You will then reverse the situation and show them the positive side of the future; how pleasant life would look, feel or sound if they take action today. You then ask them to choose which one they want. Often times, this is an "Aha Moment" for some clients.

When using pain and pleasure motivators, it is important to create equal amounts of discomfort and pleasure in order to create a balance in the visualization exercise.

Before using this tool, it is advisable to explain the process and obtain client's permission because they need to be emotionally stable to go through the process.

## Chapter 10

# Overcoming Coaching Barriers

There is no mystery about learning and understanding coaching. The truth is, coaching is not difficult to learn.

Having said that, like any other skill, the learning process requires constant practice. In life, everything is difficult until you learn and practice them. As in learning how to drive, practicing the use of coaching tools regularly will take you gradually to the point, where you become unconsciously competent to deliver breakthrough intervention without struggle.

In this Chapter, I will discuss the barriers to coaching from two different perspectives; internal barriers and external barriers.

## Internal Barriers

The greatest challenge for beginners in coaching is evidently the transition from telling, advising, counseling, and habitual teaching attitude, to asking great questions and listening patiently to clients answers. Regardless of how daunting this sounds, the good news is, even the people who thought they were not as good in practicing coaching eventually overcame their own internal barriers. If you make commitment to practice constantly with your colleagues and associates, there's no doubt you will soon become a great coach.

Sometimes, coaches are overwhelmed with the thought of what could happen during their sessions with clients. They fear they would come in contact with resisting clients or lack the ability to solve client's problems. In my opinion, these barriers exist only in the person's world of imagination.

The reality is that whoever that comes to you for coaching, must have the need to be coached in an area of life or career that is important to them. If you understood the relevant coaching tools and apply them, you should be able to deliver a great session.

It is important to acquaint yourself with the understanding that coaching is neither a problem-solving tool, nor a solution-providing kit. Although coaching results in learning, it must be clear that coaches are not teachers, and should not pretend to know the subject of coaching more than their clients.

The essence of coaching is to help clients to become **aware** of their situations, gain **understanding,** and be able to **find their own solutions**. Your role in the process is not to create the solution but take clients to the point, where they are able to find the solution they seek.

If becoming a good coach was the same as cutting down a big "Iroko" tree; and you constantly sharpened your axe before cutting begins, how long would it take you to cut down the big Iroko? The answer is only a matter of time. However, if the person chooses to focus on the size and height of the Iroko, tendency is that their *internal critics* could gain access and threaten their potential to cut down the Iroko. This is what happens when people's attention are focused attention on problems instead of solutions.

## External Barriers

External barriers are barriers other than internal barriers. They are factors existing outside the control of the coach, which are aimed at limiting his ability to coach effectively. Majority of external barriers have internal connotations, some of which include:

> Majority of the external barriers have internal connotations

## 1. Organisational culture

Some organisations resist change. They prefer the comfort of maintaining status quo. Nevertheless, dynamic leaders understood that the future of business lies in the changes they can make today. As a result, they introduce workplace coaching not as training and development program, but a major part of the overall company's culture for the benefit of both the organisation and its employees.

## 2. People resist change.

People have the tendency to resist change. But as good and useful as workplace coaching can be, management has the responsibility to decide the inclusion of coaching as an integral part of the organisation's development and growth strategy.

An important aspect of the strategy involves regular communication by senior management, of the benefits of implementing coaching as a key tool for resolving individual's and organisational challenges. This approach not only keeps the people abreast of developments, it also helps to build trust within the system; since management could be perceived as being transparent.

Naturally, people want to know the 'Why' behind their actions. A consistent open and honest conversation by way of coaching helps to explain people's "Whys" and reinforces a safe environment for them to embrace sustainable change.

## 3. It does not work

As you gradually begins to coach, it becomes possible for some of your friends and colleagues to tell you that coaching is a gimmick that does not work. Well, by now you must have known that this is not true. In reality, coaching works and if you have studied this book up to this chapter, it is possible that you have got the key facts at your finger tips to believe in the powerful of coaching. You can explain to your critics that coaching is a tested and proven tool used to improve performance and better relationship. As far as you do not give up your practice as some do, your critics will soon see the difference you make through coaching.

## 4. It's time consuming

A coaching conversation can take anything from thirty minutes to ninety minutes or more. In reality, this is long compared with the time it takes to 'tell' someone to do something. The problem is; if you tell someone what to do and he or she forgets, they will come back to ask the same question over and over, until you probably explain several times.

By explaining several times, which approach do you consider more time consuming and frustrating?

## 5. Loss of authority and control

Management-by-Coaching (MBC) is a radical departure from traditional authoritarian and control-freak approach to management. In fact, managers who manage teams by coaching are by far, more results-oriented and more respected. They have better self-esteem and make more positive impact on people's lives and society. As a result, they are more respected. What can be better than being part of the change agents that transform the world?

## 6. I'll lose my expertise

As an expert, people seek your advice and respect you for it. Adding coaching skills to what you're already doing will only add more value and increased demand for your service. Nevertheless, because coaching is neither controlling nor authoritarian, you only need to use it to *empower* others.

## 7. It's not new; I've done it before

This is an arrogant way of defending ones past failure. If someone tells you that "It's not new or they've done it before;" it's probably because they studied coaching or attended coach training classes but failed to practice it for whatever reason. Therefore seeing you coaching others only reminds them about an opportunity they lost. These people need to be coached instead. Anyone who has been involved in coaching would acknowledge the incredible transformation people and organisations experience from it.

## 8. It's hard; I won't know the questions to ask

After my first coach training class in 2009 at Gloucester Hotel London with The Coaching Academy (TCA) United Kingdom, I could barely believe how on earth I would find the questions to ask anyone to help them improve their situation. But as time went by, and I continued to practice, the barrier was broken.

If you pay attention to what your clients say, and ask a simple question to reinforce them, that alone could open up more questions for you.

Remember; your role is to help your client become awareness of their situations, and the GROW model is always there to help you. For example:

| | |
|---|---|
| **Goal** | : What do you really want? |
| **Reality** | : What is happening to you now? |
| **Options** | : What could you do? |
| **Will / Way Forward** | : What will you do now? |

To learn to become a coach and apply the skills is simple. The major obstacle lies in your ability to let go your old "Telling" habit and become more interested in asking good questions.

The process is gradual and becomes a lot easier, with a lot more opportunities opening up to you the moment you start.

# Part III
## Coaching For Performance

# Chapter 11

# Dynamics of Developing A High Performance Team

A high-performance team is a group of individuals who have come together in a work or project related circumstances; whose skills, attitudes, and competencies enable them to accomplish a common goal.

For a team to become high performing, the individual members need to posses unique qualities such as:

- ❖ Clear vision of the team's direction.
- ❖ Ability to set clear goal and take actions to achieve it.
- ❖ Ability to make tough decisions and follow through.

- ❖ Ability to hold each member accountable for their contributions towards their goals.
- ❖ Excellent robust communication skills.
- ❖ Ability to manage internal conflicts and resolve problems quickly.
- ❖ Supportive and trust-worthy disposition towards one another.
- ❖ Patience and a friendly attitude.
- ❖ Ability to commit to team objective and decisions.

A fundamental feature in developing a high performance team is the ability of team members to acknowledge their strengths and weaknesses. By so doing, they are able to compliment each other's weakness with their strengths.

Successful high-performance teams are built on a set of principles that influence their performance and underpin their actions and behaviours. They determine the extent of results they achieve both personally and for the organisations they work for.

In business, it is claimed that the success of any organisation (profit orientated or charity) is directly tied to the quality of the people it can attract, nurture, and retain at any given time. This implies that business owners and their management teams have a great deal of work of ensuring that people in their team have relevant skills and qualities that sufficiently enables them to deliver high performance results. The question is; how can management accomplish this?

## Team Development Model

The starting point in team development is for management to understand the dynamics of team development phases, and support their members to painstakingly go through the process.

In this Chapter, I will adopt a simple and easy to understand team model, which was developed in 1970 by Dr. Will Schutz at the Esalen Institute in Big Sur, California. Dr. Schutz called the model the "Firo B," after the seminar room he often used at Esalen.

Developing a high performance team with Firo B model involves three simple but important phases:

- ❖ Inclusion Phase,
- ❖ Assertion Phase, and
- ❖ Cooperation Phase.

Team members are made to go through each developmental phase until they reach the cooperation phase, which many organisations fail to reach in practice.

Firo B provides the platform for teams to demonstrate their vulnerabilities through active participation in different phases of the model until they can feel safe with their counterparts. The Manager faces the challenge of creating a safe environment that members seek. To many, this is hard work and regrettably, not always met by many managers.

In organisations where FIRO 'B' has been successfully implemented, managers and leaders have been able to build highly effective teams of high performing individuals both in sports, business and other areas of life. This Chapter will now discuss the very basics you and your colleagues can implement to achieve the same results.

## Stage 1: Inclusion Phase

This is the phase that usually determines the inclusion or otherwise of team members. It is characterized with fear, apprehension and anxiety. Think about a time you changed job to a new company; and consider how it feels hanging about without any colleague you could really trust within your first or second weeks of employment.

In the inclusion stage, people are greeted with mixed feelings. Feeling about disconnection from their friends and former colleagues in previous employment. There is also a nagging feeling about the perception and disposition of people you will meet in the new company. Even after they had made the decision to move to a new organisation, people still find themselves in a fog, with little or no idea of what could happen to them where they're going. It can be quite lonely.

Suddenly, the desperation to find new friends kicks in, and the 'fight' for inclusion and be liked begins. Productivity can be low at this level because of the unstable mindset and emotions that usually get in the way..

In order to cushion the tension, team members look up to their managers for guidance and acceptance. At this stage, the manager sets an important tone for the members. For example, if the manager is honest and shows genuine interest in supporting his team, then the fight for inclusion would be less fierce.

While it could be natural for some individuals to integrate quite easily in this phase, it could take weeks or even months for many others to feel part of the team.

## **Stage 2: Assertion Phase**

In the assertion phase, team members contest seriously for skills and recognition. The competition can get tough sometimes and reveals exceptional individual's high performance traits to the detriment of members who could not prove themselves.

The phase can be quite challenging to managers as well as some team members as they engage in disagreement with one another, including the manager sometimes. The reason is obvious; they want to validate their viewpoints and prove their skills.

Regardless of the disagreements, managers still have a duty to provide the safe environment for them to take responsibility and satisfy their assertion needs; after all, how could they work as together if they don't understand their strengths and weaknesses? This phase gives them the opportunity to discover who's who in the team.

In some cases, a great number of managers get overwhelmed by the hustling and bursting of this phase, and in attempt to keep things down, they exert their personal authority and control. Sometimes, the control-freak behaviour of some managers at this stage runs counter-productive with the objective of the assertion phase of providing a safe environment for team members to learn and understand each other's skill, strength and weakness.

It is noteworthy that team members can be quite productive in this phase of development regardless of their disagreements. But sometimes, this creates a problem for the manager, who can overlook the great potentials of individual team members as a result of too much activities going on in the team at the same time. For many organisations, the dynamic of team development stops here.

Cooperation

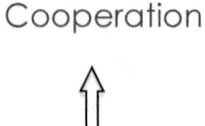

Assertion

Inclusion

## Stage 3: Cooperation Phase

It is difficult to come across high performance teams with no traits of tension. The traits notwithstanding, the underlying philosophy of team building at the cooperation phase is trust, support, encouragement and cooperation.

Unlike the assertion phase where members rejoice at the mistake of competing team members, the cooperation phase offers support and encouragement in the event that any member makes a mistake or misses his or her deadline. Consequently, if a member achieves a personal success, the rest of the team celebrates.

This is not the case with assertion phase, where member's personal achievements are greeted with jealousy from other members.

For building a team of high achievers, coaching has proven useful and highly effective. It is also highly recommended for achieving coherence in behaviour and performance, while developing team of high performers.

## Chapter 12

# Coaching Teams and Groups

In ideal situations, the responsibility of managers can be categorized into the following to aspects:

- ❖ Development of people's talents, and
- ❖ Getting the job done.

Experience shows that far too many managers are busy getting their jobs done everyday, but have shows little or no interest in developing their team's talents to improve performance.. Little wonder tough that while some organisations struggle to implement successful human capital development strategy, many others only pay a lip service to the phrase. However, with introduction of workplace coaching, it is hoped that managers will perform their entire roles more effectively and achieve better results.

In this Chapter, I am going to share the ideas about how you can build a successful team of best talents through coaching.

The focus of team coaching is not fundamentally different from everything you have learned from this book so far. Whether you are coaching individuals or team, the primary focus should be on supporting them to gain **awareness** and be able to maximise their best performance. The GROW model in Chapter 7 should always be your *guide* as you go through the process.

It is often said that first impressions matter. This is true in team coaching also. Managers have a duty to ensure that they establish the "right" connection with team members at their first meeting. It is crucial because by default, they are the team's role models. It is not a surprise that some team members adopt their manager's way of doing things; although some of them do so, only to gain the manager's favour at the inclusion phase of their development.

Managers need to be firm and focused also as what they do at this stage sets the ground rule for the team.

For example; if the manager wants the team to maintain trust, integrity, honesty and openness with one another, then he or she must demonstrate the same in their communication with the team. If they see the benefit of establishing healthy relationships outside work, or encourage outdoor engagements, it is important also that they demonstrate it as well.

> Team members see Managers as their role models.

It could be costly to under-estimate the experience, skill or quality of members of your team, especially if dealing with high performance teams. Therefore, from day one of engagement with them, be sure that what you say is consistent with what you do in the long run. If you say one thing and do another, you will no doubt encounter challenges from them.

Time is of essence in developing and coaching successful and engaged team. You need to be clear about how much time you will need to invest in building your team. It is usually ideal to set a personal goal for achieving long-term quality relationship with the team as opposed to short-term results.

As I explained in the previous chapters, FIRO 'B' model of team development, and GROW model of coaching will no doubt provide the platform and tools to move them through the various phases of development until they reach the Cooperation Phase.

## Team Coaching approaches

There are several approaches one can adopt in coaching teams. The first approach is sub-group coaching. Setting a sub-group format is useful if you are leading a fairly large team. The idea is to divide them in sub-groups of three or five members per sub-group depending on size.

The coach then asks a question and allows each sub-group to brainstorm the answer. At an appropriate time, each sub-group appoints a member, who would present their conclusion to the general team.

Once again, the GROW model will be useful for the brainstorming session. For example; based on the questions asked, you could get them to set their own **goals**. You then allow them to discuss the objectives and clearly articulate and assess the **reality** of their situations. By encouraging them to engage their creativity in finding the various **options** and deciding on the best actions for the **way forward**, their combined efforts would no doubt create the result.

During team's discussion and brainstorming exercise, it is good practice to walk around each sub-group, offering personal support or asking further questions to help them gain more awareness where necessary. Sub-group Team coaching approach requires more time than 'telling,' but if the sub-groups take responsibility and hold themselves accountable for their outcomes, performance is usually greatly enhanced.

A second approach of coaching teams is group coaching. This approach is suitable for carrying out reviews of team's past performances, or agreeing the way forward for a new goal. In a group coaching session, the manager asks a question and waits for group members to respond individually.

The question can be anything from:

- ❖ What was the most difficult part of the task for you?
- ❖ What was difficult about it?
- ❖ How long did it take to complete?
- ❖ What would you have done differently next time?
- ❖ Who needs to know about the changes you'll make?
- ❖ What support do you need, and from whom?
- ❖ If you did that, how might it affect the result or quality you'd get?
- ❖ How would that impact our work?

In group coaching, it is good idea to give members the option to respond verbally or in writing on paper. If they choose the second option, each member needs to share his or response with the rest members in the group, so they would consider each individual's input to the overall project in great detail. It will also help to clearly articulate their contributions toward the project, and increase their commitments and self-motivation.

If you or other managers in your organisation commits to building your teams in this manner; it could only take a matter of time before your organisation becomes one of best places for the best talents to work.

## Attaining Team Cooperation through Coaching

It is common for successful leaders to express concern over team's inability to take responsibility, or make strong commitment to agreed goals. This is usually an important reason for coaching in the workplace.

When coaching teams, there are quite an array of options you can adopt to successfully grow your members through to the cooperation phase. I highly recommend Sir John Whitmore's approaches, some of which are discussed below:

1. **Set common team goals**
   In many organisations, directors and chief executives determine the goals for the entire workforce.

As manager and coach, you need to further discuss the goal separately with your team, and request them to make contributions about the most effective ways for executing or dealing with it. To do this will bring clarity and foster engagement among the team; more over, when they all will be involved in taking actions toward reaching the goal.

2. **Set the ground rules**

   Ground rules are like values and beliefs. They regulate the conducts and behaviours of team members towards one another as they work through the process of achieving the goal together.

   The rules need to be clearly stated, understood, agreed, and complied with by all members. This makes it possible for members to respect one another's opinions or viewpoints, and also understand the clear boundaries for team success.

   As the team makes progress with the goal, the manager needs to ensure that the ground rules are being adhered to; and also determine when it becomes due for update.

3. **Understand your team's values**

    Your can grow your team's performance exponentially if you make effort to understand what gives meaning to their lives. *Values* and *mission (Purpose)* are at the core of people's performance in any field of endeavour. They contribute extensively in shaping people's behaviour and response to issues.

    If your team's goal is not aligned with individual member's values and purpose, there is possibility they would perform poorly, Over a long period of time, it could lead to resignation from the team or employment.

    Discovering team member's values requires commitment. Generally, holding individual or collective team meeting with a view to examining the factors that drive their behaviour has proven successful in many organisations.. Nevertheless, It does not make any sense to only identify people's values without acknowledging and reinforcing them. By acknowledging and reinforcing people's values, they feel a sense of respect and importance, all of which contribute to improved performance.

4. **Set up a support system**
   Sometimes, situations arise that make even high achievers to doubt their self-esteem, lose enthusiasm and get involved in conflict with others. In order to minimize this type of situation in a team, it's important to consider setting up a support system that will deal with dysfunctions in teams. This would significantly protect team's morale and strengthen their self-esteem.

It is important to bear in mind also that your role as coach is not to fix your team's problems. As you transform from managing to coaching, you no longer need to impose your personal *will* and *authority* on your team (clients). Instead, your actions will henceforth be focused towards helping them to achieve their team objectives, which is primarily to improve performance.

# Chapter 13

# Giving Constructive Feedback And Carrying Out Assessment

Constructive feedback is useful for self-development. In a work environment, it provides useful ongoing guidance through supply of information to support effective behaviour, or to provide direction for someone to get back on tract and improve his or her performance. Without feedback, people hardly tell whether they or someone else are on course in what they are doing.

A good feedback system should neither be judgmental nor used for faultfinding. In reality, many managers give feedback in ways that hurt their subordinates thereby making the tool highly ineffective for performance improvement in their organisations. In this Chapter, I am going to share with you, how coaching can be used as a useful tool for giving feedback and carrying out assessment.

Over the course of many years of working with managers and leaders of small and medium size businesses, as well as large organisations, I have observed various ways people give feedback (consciously or unconsciously) to their colleagues.

Let us examine the following five real life feedback examples in great detail:

1. **You are useless**
   This is a direct personal criticism on an individual, aimed at destroying his or her self-confidence. This type of statement is not helpful for growth or development as it makes the individual's performance even worse.

2. **Your report is useless**

   The statement is a judgmental feedback directed not at the individual but his or her output. The implication is the same as if it were directed to the person because it destroys his or her confidence and self-esteem.

3. **Some information on your report is valid, but the arrangement is messy.**

   By all means, this gives some forms of knowledge to the person addressed, which can be worked on. However, It does not give enough detail about what should be improved. The feedback, even though not criticizing is not helpful for the individual's development.

4. **How do you feel about your output?**

   This feedback shifts ownership to the individual by asking about his or her opinion on their output. The problem it is that it does not engage the individual in any meaningful discussion, or elicit useful response from them. The best anybody can get from this type of closed question is: "Fine," "Great," "Good," or "Not too great." It does not make room for improvement.

5. **What primary objective does your report aim at, and to what extent was it met? What else needs to be highlighted?**

   These is a non-judgmental feedback in question format. The statements offer the individuals opportunity to think through, evaluate their actions, and assess what was missing (if any). By all standards, this type of feedback is constructive and suitable for performance improvement.

Here are some of the important lessons you can learn from the statements above. Particularly for the fifth one; the manager's objective was for the individual to recall his or her *understanding* about the primary objective of producing the report. It also involves assessing the extent to which the objective was met. It goes further to remind them to check if any information was missing from the report.

This is what a good workplace coaching session essentially seeks to achieve through feedback. Rather than *telling* the individual what he or she did right or wrong, the manager engages in a conversation that opens possibilities to evaluate their performance by themselves. By this, the individual is empowered to **take ownership** of his or her work, gain much more understanding, and increase their self-confidence.

## Commend – Recommend – Commend (CRC) Principle

In my role as past Vice President Education (VPE) of Cambridge Speakers Club - a Toastmasters International Club in United Kingdom; I learned what I thought was one of the most effective ways of giving feedback. In Toastmasters, we call it "Commend – Recommend – Commend" (CRC).

After listening to a member's speech, someone stands in the crowd and evaluates the speech in CRC format. In doing this, we ensure that our members are fed back positively. We do not look for errors or mistakes; instead we look out for opportunities for our members to improve their speaking skills. Even though we evaluate every speech, we are careful about our choice of word, and do not use phrases such as "criticism," "error" or "mistake."

Instead,

- ❖ We listen and observe the speaker to identify skills he or she already has, which they can use again, and commend them for using such skills.

- ❖ We recommend ways the speaker could improve his or her existing skills and overcome any observed weaknesses.

- ❖ We then wrap up by encouraging the speaker to book more slots in future meetings, and tell them how desperately we're looking forward to hear them speak again.

In a nutshell, Toastmaster's evaluation feedback takes the format below:

1. Give up to three commendations.
2. Give up to two recommendations.
3. Wrap up with any other strongest commendation you can find.

What I discovered from giving feedback both at Toastmasters, corporate organisations, and anywhere people requested me to do so, is that feedback stimulates learning and improves performance.

Particularly in Toastmaster's club, if an evaluator observes that a speaker did not make adequate use of the stage, he could say something like, **"I observed that you had such massive space at your disposal and I expected that you could just have fun with it."** Another way someone could approach the same matter could be: "…unfortunately you did not make use of the stage space which, I guess contributed to your inability to express yourself well enough during your speech." The difference is clear isn't it?

## Who takes ownership of the problem?

I believe that Toastmasters International is a personal development platform for professionals who are constantly seeking to improve their public speaking skills. As a result member's feedback and evaluations are taken very seriously.

Notwithstanding, there were instances where few members displayed defensive behaviour during their evaluations. They refused to accept their evaluator's comments; instead they gave tons of excuses to justify what they did. This is not a good way of learning for performance improvement, and given the circumstance, any further feedback would only result in argument and bad feeling. Coaching therefore provides a better approach for dealing with situations such as this.

Let me buttress my point further.

Supposing I was coaching the same speaker, whom it was observed, did not make adequate use of space on the stage, I could say something like:

> "James, I noticed you did not make enough use of the stage space while speaking, what do you think was responsible for your action?"

Notice that I made the same observation the evaluator made previously. What I did differently was leaving ownership of the problem entirely with the James.

Sometimes, people take ownership of other people's problems and challenges by simply assuming they understood their issues. They tell, give advice, make suggestions, and offer counsel about what they believe the other person should do. We see this happen in feedback and evaluation activities.

But with coaching, clients are given total control of the issues (goals). The coach is not a teacher and does not tell clients what to do. Coaching simply opens up the situation, and empowers clients to think through other various ways they could resolve their issues. By this means, the client retains total control of not only the problems that brought them to coaching, but the solutions also.

The process helps clients to reflect on their actions - what they did, and be able to consider what they can do differently next time. It helps them create awareness that leads to learning, which automatically increases performance.

AWARENESS ⇒ LEARNING ⇒ PERFORMANCE

Feedback does not need to be given only on individual's accomplishments, but on the process the individuals adopted in accomplishing the tasks also.

In above example, the speech was the outcome, and the fact that the speaker (probably) stood just still without making enough body language to engage his or her audience was all part of the process. Too often, people judge the outcome of an action without giving consideration to the process that created the outcome, thereby eliciting defensive reasoning and undue justifications.

## Appraisal System

Truth is, we cannot fully understand an outcome if we do not examine the actions that led to the outcome. From my personal experience of coaching and giving feedback to successful entrepreneurs, corporate executives and professionals; only the client has exclusive understanding of the actions that created their outcomes.

As a result, their personal feedback will be so powerful in producing sustainable learning for them. I believe this is what creates peak performance in the long run.

Here's another thought for you. Traditionally, an organisation's effectiveness can be evaluated by examining the Strengths and Weaknesses of its workforce. That's what many companies do with SWOT Analysis. As part of the feedback loop, they could decide to make a list of skills, qualities, and behaviours, which they consider fundamental for their organisation's success.

These skills, qualities and behaviours can then serve as benchmark for staff in the different business units of the organisation such as administrations, finance, customer service, or IT. By clearly identifying the skills in various units, staff member's strengths and weaknesses can then be evaluated on a scale of, say 1 to 10 to measure what's working and what needs to be improved.

When skills and potentials are clearly broken down, and individuals are made aware of management's expectations on them; coaching can then be used to build the capacity for meeting those expectations. This process can be achieved in conjunction with a good appraisal system.

A good appraisal system therefore, is another great human capital development tool that evaluates employee's performance and provides feedback for improvement. It is designed to capture past performances as well as individual's potentials, which are required for constantly reaching the organisation's vision.

A well-designed appraisal system can be effective for carrying out self-assessment. The table below shows how self-assessment can contribute to learning and high performance in combination with appraisal.

|  | Where I am Now | Where I want to be |
|---|---|---|
| Trust | 8 | 10 |
| Communication | 7 | 10 |
| Confidentiality | 8 | 10 |
| Patience | 6 | 10 |
| Presentation | 5 | 10 |

Self-assessment eliminates criticisms and empowers individuals to take a hard look on their performance with a view to identifying areas of further improvement. It raises individual's awareness to the reality of skills they presently have, and the improvements they might need to reach future expectations.

Having objectively placed an individual's skillset on a scale of 1 to 10, the next stage in the process is to carefully choose which skills need to be developed further. Looking at the table above, the individual on scale 5 can be coached through to scale 6 until he or she reaches 10 out of 10, which is the organisation's benchmark.

Appraisal and self-assessment systems can also be useful in team setting, where employees need to assess themselves against qualities and behaviours desired by management for performing certain roles, or attaining specific levels of promotion within the organisation. Where disparities exist in a desirable quality, the manager has a responsibility to coach the individual to close the disparity.

Generally speaking, coaching can be very useful for developing human talents and increasing performance in business, workplace, and other areas of human endeavour.

# Coaching Toolkit

This section of the book deals with tools, exercises and other support systems, which you and other coaches can find useful for helping your clients to make progress in any areas of their lives and career.

We do not believe in the popular saying that: "Practice makes perfect." Instead, on the basis of our experience of working with, and supporting many successful business owners and executives including individuals society had once written off; we have developed new beliefs, one of which is that: "Practice only makes progress."

Experienced coaches all over the world use different types of tools and exercises with their clients.

Our desire is to share some of our tried and tested tools, which have been widely used by successful coaches with you, so you continue to practice with them and experience progressive progress in your career..

These tools have been designed in downloadable format. All you need to do is visit our website at www.cognitionglobal.com/taaf and download them.

We hope to continue to update the and add new ones as they become available.

1. 40 GROW Question (10 questions per GROW segment)
2. Life Wheel
3. SWOT for Business
4. SWOT for Personal Development
5. Time Management Matrix
6. Client/Coachee Contact Chart
7. Personal Development Tool
8. Tool for Taking Responsibility
9. What I want Tool
10. Business Planning Tool

# About The Author

**Nkem Paul** is a devout Christian, an experienced entrepreneur, a qualified business coach, and author. Nkem has passion for entrepreneurship, leadership, and high performance.

His background is as Chartered Accountant with nearly 20 years of practical experience at senior levels in bank and other financial institutions in Africa and United Kingdom.

Presently, Nkem works with successful entrepreneurs and corporate executives, helping them to develop capacity to multiply opportunities and double profitability. He is President of Cognition Global Concepts Limited, and founder of Yodel Business School Cambridge.

## Other Books By The Author